Rough Meditations

Bradley S. Klein

SLEEPING BEAR PRESS

Sleeping Bear Press
121 South Main
P.O. Box 20
Chelsea, MI 48118

Sleeping Bear Ltd.
7 Medallion Place
Maidenhead, Berkshire
England

Printed and bound in Canada by Friesen's, Altona, Manitoba.

10 9 8 7 6 5 4 3 2 1

Cataloging-in-Publication Data
    Klein, Bradley S.
        Rough meditations / Bradley S. Klein
            p. cm.
        Includes bibliographical references (p.)
        ISBN 1-886947-17-1
            1. Golf courses—Design and construction. 2. Golf. I. Title.
    GV975.K53   1997
    796.352'06'8—dc21   97-2467
                                                             CIP

Cover photo: The Pete Dye Golf Club, Bridgeport, WV, courtesy of Mark Brown/ Golf Stock Inc.

Rough
Meditations

Contents

Acknowledgments

Nothing of the work that appears in this book would have been possible had Herbert Warren Wind not kindly left the press tent at the 1979 U.S. Open to see me after I had a security guard deliver a letter to him. The ensuing correspondence meant a lot during the days when editors' rejection letters were commonplace.

A longstanding friendship with Canadian writer Lorne Rubenstein has proved at least as meaningful—and at levels that go far beyond mere golf.

I am grateful to *GolfWeek*, *iGolf*, *Links* magazine, and *Score* for permission to draw upon material that first appeared in these publications. "Caddying for Pat Ward-Thomas at the Old Course" first appeared in *Golf Journal* (January–February 1987); "Golf and the Environment" in *Met Golfer* (April–May 1995); and "Scotland's Northern Links" in *Golf for Women* (February 1994, © Meredith Corporation). I appreciate the publishers' permission to include these here.

When the first of my essays was published, our daughter, Cory-Ellen Nadel, was two years old. Now she's a college freshman who puts my grammar and vocabulary to shame.

Finally, to Jane Nadel-Klein, my wife, best friend, and most ruthless editor. The night we met she asked, "What is there to write about golf?" The following pages are a partial answer.

Introduction

Back in high school my friends and parents used to laugh at me when I told them I enjoyed caddying. They saw it as work, whereas I saw it as time spent outdoors on beautiful land. All through high school my version of doodling took the form of sketches of my favorite golf holes. At one point I started doing full routings on sheets of oak tag paper, and then played a complicated dice game on them that I had devised. Given my own very shaky game of golf it was the closest I would ever get to regularly shooting in the 70s.

Soon, however, I gave up the dice game. Not, however, the fascination with golf holes and golf courses. I discovered a rich literature on the subject and began to study maps and illustrations of famous holes. When the chance came in the mid-1970s to caddie on the PGA Tour, well, I couldn't wait to see the world's best players on the world's finest layouts.

And so was born *Rough Meditations*. To be sure, it took another 20 years before the essays were in place, but the essential vision has been with me for some time now. The point of these various pieces is to convey how lovely, even mysterious, golf courses are, and at the same time to explain—without getting overly technical—how they got to be that way.

This is, in effect, a user's guide, intended to help those of us who play golf to appreciate the ground we walk—or ride—on. Will it make you a better player? Actually it will, because the reader who takes the golf course seriously will adapt his or her game to the lay of the land and to the demands of its peculiar features.

But I didn't write this strictly, or narrowly, as an instructional aid. This is more an attempt to help other golfers appreciate the aesthetics of the most interesting playing fields in all of sports. It's also intended to help private club members and daily-fee golfers to make more informed judgments about their home courses and to explain how those layouts might be preserved or enhanced. Finally, it is intended to evoke a certain classical tradition and respect for the game's heritage. This is, after all, a sport that started centuries ago along the coast and that has now spread throughout the world to every imaginable landscape. Perhaps after reading this book, you'll appreciate even more the places you frequent. Perhaps, too, you'll be motivated to travel and study the game's roots and to experience firsthand golf's great landmarks, both in North America and wherever in the world the game has exercised its powerful hold.

This is an era in which golf enjoys immense popularity. The emergence of Tiger Woods to international stardom will only help draw more people to the first tee. My own sense, discovered in the 1960s and renewed ever since all over the world, is that paying close attention to the landforms we play golf on makes the game even more enchanting and more fun. It also helps you think your way around the golf course. Most importantly, it establishes a connection between the present and the past. Those are precisely the kinds of cultural links that make golf a compelling sport. Perhaps these rough meditations will help explain why.

1

Early Days

Father's Day

My father, Milton, has never been a sports fan, certainly not by the time I was growing up in ticky-tacky suburban Queens, New York. He is a first-generation American, the son of Jewish immigrants who came over in 1905 from some hopeless field of mud in a Polish shtetl—a town called Orla. There was no sandlot baseball played there, nor a round of golf—not even to this day. Instead, there were more important things to be done, like eking out a living. The same work ethic prevailed in the New World as my grandfather opened up a dry cleaning store in Brooklyn—horse-drawn delivery and all.

My father's life has included Brooklyn Tech, the Cooper Union, and a passing interest in the Dodgers, but never to the point where he attended Ebbets Field. In what came to be the paradigm for our own relationship, it was I, in 1964, who took him to his first baseball game; a freezing but exciting Thursday night game at Shea Stadium, two days after the All-Star game, with the Mets winning 5-4 in the bottom of the ninth with a 2-out, 3-run home run by Frank Thomas. Not that I remember much, or that such details betray any significance.

Throughout high school, I caddied at various Long Island clubs—Woodmere, Inwood, Lawrence, and my favorite layout, Rockaway Hunting Club, which was my first exposure to linksland golf. Occasionally, very rarely indeed, I gathered up the courage to ask my father for a lift. This was still in the days when you had to provide your own means of transport or not go at all, and so most of the time I either bicycled the eight or so miles or took the Long Island Railroad.

The best part of caddying was playing on Mondays, and I made generous use of the privilege. Once, on a sweltering hot summer evening, I persuaded my folks to come with me—by then, I could drive—and they joined me for a few holes along the inlet known as Broswere Bay, where the Rockaway Hunting Club turned magical. On the sixth fairway, I handed my father a five-iron, dropped a ball, and asked him to hit. He flailed away, made contact, walked over to the ball and hit it again. This went on for a few minutes, and then he handed the club back to me, satisfied that he had fulfilled his paternal obligation. "Enough," he said.

But it wasn't.

☙

Return to Inwood

We used to drive past a beautiful-looking golf course on the way to Rockaway Beach, touring about in our '57 Studebaker, and then after that, a '63 Dodge Dart. As we passed by, I would crane my neck and look out the back window. It turned out to be Inwood Country Club.

I had never seen a piece of land as beautiful. A wrought iron fence surrounded the grounds, setting it off from a series of dilapidating single family houses. Traffic breezed by, making the stately parkland site all the more intriguing. So one summer morning, I would guess when I was nine years old, I headed off on my bicycle and an hour later found myself at its gates.

It was something out of a movie, or better yet, the cover of one of those Hardy Boy books I had at home, with me standing there, looking up at this massive stone entranceway, and deep inside the grounds was this spooky, old-fashioned clubhouse. Beneath the metal plate announcing "Inwood Country Club" was a warning about "Private: Members Only." All of this was too inviting for me to turn back now. My sole act of deference was to get off my bike and to walk it up the private road.

Various groups of people stood around in the distance—golfers, accompanied by caddies. Dense shades of green were everywhere, all of it framed by graceful trees and some lovely shrubbery and flower beds. It all seemed in such contrast to the world I had passed through to get here. I thought it best to avoid the clubhouse because there was no way I was going to be able to explain away my visit if any member confronted me. Just as the path climbed up to the clubhouse, I veered off to the right and headed down behind the parking lot. There I found a spot behind some bushes and left my bicycle unlocked.

On one side stretched the swamps of Jamaica Bay, and across the water were the main runways of Idlewild—later John F. Kennedy—Airport. To my right was a row of hedges, and just beyond it unfolded this huge expanse of lawn and trees. We had a black and white television at home, and the only other time I remember being overwhelmed like this was when I first watched a baseball game on a neighbor's color set. It wasn't just the size of the yard here, it was also the intensity of the green color and all the shades and varieties, and the way the branches draped so lovingly over everything. I walked down by a putting surface, headed across a little stone bridge that carried me over a lily pond, and then walked along one side of a fairway back toward a group of golfers.

Way in the distance, I saw someone swing. The metal shaft glinted, the ball rose against the blue sky, and then I heard a kind of "click" sound as the ball headed right at me, except that it gently climbed, then leveled off and floated, seemingly forever. By the time the ball butterflied down to earth in front of me, I had fallen in love with the game.

More than 25 years later I returned to Inwood CC, this time with our 11-year-old daughter, Cory, in hand, to show her the spot where my fascination with golf had started. Like my father, she had done a good job of playing along with my interest, at one point even taking up the game as a way of spending time with me. She could even watch it on TV with me and began to register a certain familiarity with players. So I thought it a good idea one morning while we visited my parents to conjure yet another reason for an early morning escape.

She was always quick to join a conspiracy, and so we set off together in my '90 Toyota Tercel.

The ride didn't seem nearly as long this time. Strange, how age shrinks distance. The buildings along the way all looked a little smaller than they had been when I was growing up. The roads were more packed with chintzy businesses, neon signs, and the general sense of nowhere that has become typical of strip-mall culture. But then I made the right turn off Sheridan Boulevard and it all came back to me just as it had been, replete with the empty sand lot in front of the country club and the sign reminding me that I didn't belong.

This time, though, there was nothing to hide. One key to American society, I have learned, is that if you act as if you belong, people will play along. It's just a matter of knowing how to look like you're part of what's going on. This time I parked close to the clubhouse, waved a friendly greeting to the doorman, and then headed off with Cory to the pro shop, where we introduced ourselves to the resident professional. Tommy Thomas, his name was, and I had known him tangentially from my caddie days on the PGA Tour several summers earlier. He had been one of the many journeyman golfers who tries his hand at the big life and then finds out for all sorts of reasons that he just can't quite compete or that life on the road is too demanding. In any case, I remembered him not for any success he enjoyed—on the contrary—but for his trademark use of a certain suspect golf ball: "the Molitor man," he been called, and now, some 12 years later, he smiled when I recalled this nickname. There is no escaping a nickname on The Tour.

In brief compass, we divested ourselves of our limited supply of shared Tour memories. "Would it be okay if we headed off to the 18th hole? I want to show Cory here where I . . . well, where I first discovered golf." "Sure," he said, "just make sure you stay out of the way of any play. We have a few early birds; they went off the back nine and may be finishing already."

This time, the grounds took on a meaning that had not been available to me in my youth. Inwood Country Club, after all, had been the site of two major golf championships, the 1921 PGA and the 1923 U.S. Open. That stone bridge fronting the green was copied from the famous original on the 18th hole at the Old Course at St. Andrews. I recounted this to Cory as we walked down the right side of the 18th fairway.

It was a lovely day, the air warming up, the sky clear, and none of those noisy airplanes disturbing the morning calm. And as we walked over and stood on the exact spot where so many years ago I had begun my affair with the game, I turned around and saw a historic marker that, I later found out, had only recently been placed there in the ground. "In 1923, Bobby Jones clinched the first of his four U.S. Open titles by hitting a two-iron from this spot to within six feet of the hole during a playoff with Bobby Cruickshank."

Cory read the marker aloud without really understanding it. She did, however, understand what the moment meant to me. This 11-year-old, who usually talked for hours without coming up for air, stood quietly by my side for a few minutes while I relived all the emotions of my first visit.

Then she looked up at me, and with utter seriousness in her gray eyes, said, "Cool."

2

Caddying

Stand by Your Man

So, my player has missed the cut again. I'm disappointed, but not surprised. Obviously, I had little confidence in him. After his opening 77, I signed out of the hotel before coming to the course on Friday morning. Still, this latest disaster is almost more than I can bear. He was beginning to make a comeback on the course, but a three-putt green on the back nine secured the fate that I had feared. I sit there wondering how I can continue to take caddying seriously.

Yet I keep returning to the job. With this, the '81 Canadian Open, I'll have worked the tournament five consecutive years. With four different players, two of them top money winners, I have yet to survive the 36-hole cut. But I am not discouraged by this track record. Nor am I a masochist. There is something about the game, even about caddying, that calls me back for more.

During most of the year I work toward my Ph.D. and teach political science at the University of Massachusetts. Literally the day classes are over, though, I get on a bus, or sometimes on an airplane, and head south to join the professional golf tour as a regular caddie for the late spring and summer months. I arrange with a player weeks in advance to have a job awaiting me when I get into town. Often I have to grade final exams in my motel room. One year I had to edit my advisor's manuscript in my motel room while caddying down in Texas. My colleagues often ask me if my caddying interferes with my studies. "Of course not," I tell them, " though my studies usually interfere with my caddying." They think I'm kidding.

Why caddie on tour? Well, it helps a lot if you love the game. If you have spent the cold New England winter watching tournaments on television and kept track of golf statistics like a little leaguer who studies baseball cards; if you read up on golf history and course architecture and play golf like I do— despite your swing—then there is nothing more thrilling than working week after week at the side of a touring pro. You travel. You see the country. You're inside the ropes on the finest golf courses you've only read about. And you are able to experience a very different lifestyle.

For me it started as a country club "looper" on Long Island: 36 holes, two bags, every weekend I could. Throughout high school in New York City I caddied at the Woodmere Club, and with aid from the Long Island Caddie Scholarship Fund I attended the State University of New York at Binghamton. In those days, the B.C. Open, now a significant tour stop, was just getting off the ground at a municipal course in Endicott, New York, on which I occasionally played. Working that tournament after my graduation not only relieved the agony of unemployment, it was also my first taste of big-time golf. My player, Dick Rhyan, qualified on Monday, made the cut with ease, and then collapsed over the weekend to win $452. I was hooked on the job.

Most people start caddying as a temporary job. The work begins to overwhelm you, though, especially if you work for a contender. I once worked for Lon Hinkle at Pinehurst No. 2. The first three days he shot 65-67-69. No, he did not win the tournament. But it is golf like that, observed firsthand, that keeps a caddie on the road.

The very origins of the word "caddie" give a clue to the bag-toter's function on the golf course. The term is the Scottish spelling of the French term "cadet." Cadets were young, unskilled, but aspiring soldiers. Their initiation into military life consisted of accompanying to battle the more experienced cavalrymen. Cadets in both France and Great Britain assisted in carrying and reloading arms, but did not themselves do battle. These cadets, like the tour caddies today, served quietly in the face of battle, enduring without glory their temporary subordinate status.

The job appears simple, but when you are on the back nine of the fourth round, tension and excitement begin to overtake you. This "being in the hunt" isn't found at an office desk. Add national television, 30,000 spectators, and a bag full of money behind the 18th green, and you are likely to want to stay. You will put in more hours than on a 9-to-5 job, but the freedom and thrill it affords you are extraordinary.

People from all sorts of backgrounds are drawn into caddying. One fellow quit a lucrative attorney's position to come out on tour. Several others completed graduate studies in accounting, math, and law. For years, a New Jersey high school principal spent his summers working for Kathy Whitworth on the LPGA Tour. On the men's tour today one finds quiet family men, ex-felons, frustrated golf pros, a meteorologist, former prize fighters, real estate brokers, and an alcoholic or three.

Not everyone finds success on the golf circuit. Many bounce around for years, hoping to catch a young player on the rise with whom a partnership can be built. Mike ("Fluff") Cowan, one of the best golfers among the caddies, worked for a succession of apparently talented young players who for years went absolutely nowhere. Usually penniless, Mike drove around the tour in a broken-down green Chevy van. If you got a ride with "Fluff," you paid for both the gas bill and his hamburger breakfasts. Finally, Mike hitched up with Peter Jacobsen. After two shaky years, Jacobsen broke through as a winner in the tournament—the Buick Open—where Mike's caddie career had begun four years earlier. Everybody on tour dreams of such a breakthrough. But for every one like Cowan who works his way up from nowhere there are a dozen others left behind with nothing to show for their efforts.

My own motives for caddying have nothing to do with building a career on tour. To be sure, I harbor visions of carrying that bag down the final hole with my player's name atop the scoreboard. The money also helps me through the summer months. The difference, however, is that I've never sought a livelihood out there. If that has kept me from getting a steady job with a Nicklaus, Trevino, or Crenshaw, it surely has never diminished my enthusiasm about the player for whom I do work.

On the golf course and in motels, restaurants, and of course, in late-night bars, the caddies relate to one another in terms that have little to do with their backgrounds. They will initiate you into their traveling circus world with a nickname that captures your essence. I happen to be "Professor." One also finds "Gypsy," "Disco," "Gorgeous George," "Beer Can Louie," "Rabbit," and "Killer" (the former boxer who, thankfully, as Hale Irwin's longtime caddie, does not live up to this name). With this colorful crew you will get into conversations about every imaginable topic: golf lore, horse racing, rock music, and, lest we forget, women.

You can set these issues aside, however, when you step onto the golf course. Here only one thing counts. Are you just a "bag-toter" or are you really a caddie? With a player's bag upon your shoulder it matters not whether you are illiterate or a former Member of Parliament. The decisive issue is simply whether you know your way around a golf course.

A bag-toter dumbly carries the clubs around and knows as much about the game as a donkey knows about the load he drags. But a caddie! Well, a caddie can talk up a storm about the difference between bent grass and Bermuda greens. He knows the yardage between any two points on every golf course he has set foot upon. When the player knocks his five-iron shot on the green, the caddie will recall from last year's tournament how that putt should break. He can also describe ad nauseam every shot he has seen since the 1962 Texas Open.

A caddie remembers every dime owed to him and each percentage check he has ever endorsed. He is also likely to think his player incapable of winning without listening to his own precious instruction. The caddie might not have much of a bank account, and his cockiness is markedly diminished when in the company of his player. Put him in a Wednesday pro-am, however, and he'll teach those amateurs how to hit cut shots out of fairway bunkers and to line up 40-foot putts that cannot help but go in. In short, a caddie knows his golf.

Despite their cultivated expertise, the caddies are a sullen crew. Their destiny is precarious; success depends not on their own knowledge but upon the uses to which it is put by their player. There can be no escaping this dilemma. The only measure of a good caddie is the good scoring of his player. For the most part, then, a caddie's mood is determined by his player's recent fate; his alternating depression and elation corresponds to the position of his player on the scoreboard. No caddie, however thoughtful, is entirely immune from this affliction.

A caddie's life is neither secure nor very luxurious. All the caddies pay their own expenses. With hotels, meals, gasoline, and laundry this can easily run several hundred dollars per week. Though many caddies can live for less, their appearance, diet, health, and police records are bound to suffer accordingly. It is not uncommon, for instance, to find four impoverished "bag rats" camping out in a room designed for, and rented to, one.

Virtually no caddies have written contracts: 99 percent of them are hired—and fired—on the basis of oral agreements (which, as the saying goes, are not worth the paper they are written on), and nobody gets a 10 percent tip unless it is on a win.

For a long time, the caddies were treated by the PGA Tour's field staff and by most of the tournament sponsors as public nuisances to be kept out of the way. With a few notable exceptions, such as at the B.C. Open in upstate New York, we are persona non grata, if not the object of scorn. Some tournament sites are marginally better than others. One week the caddies have convenient parking privileges and free lunches; the next week, it is back to normal with parking half a mile from the clubhouse and the sponsors insisting we wear bulky and insufferably hot overalls that carry the player's name on the back.

The clubhouse is definitely off limits, even when you are finished working for the week. Caddies who need to run errands for their players are not allowed in the locker room. And at nearly every club the caddies are continually hassled by marshals and security guards. Usually, the most helpful people are the regular club employees working in the bag room. Otherwise, the caddies fight a quiet running battle with officialdom everywhere. A caddie's life is hectic. It is also parasitic upon the public glamour of the tour.

The demands made upon tour caddies are more varied than their pay. Some golfers demand that their caddies stand by the bag every Tuesday while they learn how to fade a three-iron. Tom Kite's caddie is not the only one accustomed to seeing sunset on the driving range. Some are required to survey the course every morning of a tournament round to ascertain new pin placements.

Other responsibilities are not strictly golf related. Some

caddies drive their player's car from tournament to tournament (a benefit actually, since free transportation is thus provided). A few have been known to arrange dates for their golfers with attractive women in the gallery. Some will even meet their player's girlfriend at the airport in the middle of the night.

A caddie, then, is paid not only to carry the clubs but to keep a watchful eye on all aspects of the game. He is valet, chauffeur, procurer, and panderer.

Psychologist, too. He must instill confidence and security in his player. The caddie's true worth is that inchoate dimension of support he provides under tournament pressure. In playing the final nine holes on Sunday, a day on which fortunes are made and careers are made or broken, a player under pressure cannot afford to worry whether his caddie will stomp all over his putting line, give him bad yardage, or "choke" when asked whether the shot calls for a six- or seven-iron.

The caddie and the player must work together, quietly but securely. When Tom Watson approaches the green he is surveying his shot. There is no need for him to turn around in search of his caddie or to ask for his putter. He walks, holds out his hand, and Bruce Edwards has the club waiting for him. A good caddie, knowing his player well, anticipates his needs.

The partnership between player and caddie is not, however, an equal one. Certainly the player has the toughest job. A confident caddie knows that his player "pulls the trigger," while he must stand aside and watch. The golfer bears the burden of public scrutiny while the caddie awaits helplessly and mutters to himself a silent secular prayer. But the sense of despair, hope, and urgency that overcomes one as the ball is in the air can be moderated by the assurance that the element of chance has been minimized. All factors cannot possibly be accounted for in advance. This is precisely the beauty and uniqueness of the game. A bad swing, an unlucky bounce, a sudden gust of wind can never be foreseen. All that a caddie can do for his golfer is reduce the number of unknown factors.

When your player asks for the yardage or the wind direction, you must know exactly, and answer without hesitation. You must anticipate, react, and offer advice without equivocation. There is no time out there for a seminar discussion. The player only wants to hear what you know.

It is not that golf is thoughtless. Quite the contrary, it requires intense concentration and reflection. But in a professional tournament, with the stakes so high, a means must be found to impose an artifice of certainty upon what is at best an elusive, uncertain endeavor.

I make no pretension to golf's secret affinity with the nature of academic life. That I find joy and meaning in both is reason enough for me to continue. Perhaps here I share much in common with the average sports fan. A sport, a game, is by nature confined. It makes no claim to truth. It simply arouses us by the sheer beauty of its motion. The strength that it calls for, the careful design of its playing field in distinct isolation from the everyday world: these are the sources of its appeal.

ᨳ

A Brief History of Caddying

On the morning of the second qualifying round for the 1932 British Open, the American golfing great, Gene Sarazen, looked out from his hotel window overlooking the Royal St. George's course and saw his caddie, Skip Daniels, already on the links. No, Sarazen hadn't missed his starting time. Rather, his caddie was out there all huddled up in his raincoat, fighting through the wind of a gale, in order simply to take note of that day's pin placements.

The story goes that as Sarazen looked out upon the golf course, he thought to himself, "If Daniels is working this hard for me, I'll have to work that hard for him." Sarazen went on to win the tournament, a victory he credits in part to his caddie's counsel. For Daniels, who had earlier caddied for and won with Walter Hagen, it was to be his last British Open. He died early the next spring. But Sarazen never forgot him. Skip Daniels, the classic rough-hewn, slightly grizzled elder caddie, had stood faithfully by his man.

The earliest golf art portraying the gentry on the links frequently shows a young lad carrying clubs over his shoulder. The golf bag, now a basic piece of equipment, did not appear until the late 1800s. As for the caddies themselves, the first one whose name has come down to us is Andrew Dickson, caddie to the Duke of York in 1681 and 1682. A later memoir testifies, however, that Dickson, like many caddies over the next two centuries, not only carried the clubs, he manufactured them as well. There wasn't enough money in caddying by which to earn a living, and though young lads could pick up a few pence here and there, it was not uncommon to find caddies also employed as local golf instructors. Indeed, they were skilled in all arts of the game. Such was the status of David Robertson at St. Andrews in the early 1800s: club maker, ball maker, and "oldest of the cads."

A number of the world's finest players refined their golfing skills by way of the caddie ranks. Allan Robertson, David Robertson's son, started as a caddie and became the game's first full-time professional player. For those born into less fortunate golfing circumstances, entry to the game has only been possible via the caddie yard. Gene Sarazen started in golf by caddying to earn spare money. Ben Hogan and Byron Nelson played their first golf on "caddie's day" in Forth Worth, Texas. And two recent European stars, Seve Ballesteros and Bernhard Langer, were only able to begin playing because of their youthful employment as caddies.

Sadly, the days of the caddie have faded. The virtual demise of the club caddie is due entirely to the golf cart. Actually, it was the hand-pulled "trolley" of the early twentieth century that first challenged the caddie's craft. But with the advent of the motorized golf cart after World War II, the attractions of not having to walk seemed to exercise a decisive hold over golfers of certain nationalities—particularly in the U.S., where club managers and professionals seized the opportunity to reap considerable profits renting gas and electric powered carts.

By the 1970s, fewer than one in ten private clubs in North America had anything resembling a caddie crew. Caddies now tend to be found at only the most exclusive clubs, and it is still not uncommon, especially in the American deep south, to see an all-black caddie crew tending to an all-white membership. Augusta National in Georgia, the site of the annual Masters tournament each April, was so persistent in this regard that until 1983 it banned the regular tour caddies from the tournament and allowed only its local (black) caddies to work there.

A modest effort is underway in the States to bring back the caddie. Regional golf associations, working with certain clubs, have sponsored training workshops in caddying, and a few clubs—East Lake in Atlanta, Bloomfield Hills north of Detroit, Inverness in Toledo—not only make caddies available but virtually require that members take a caddie rather than a cart. In order to assure work to those caddies who do show up, many clubs now require that one caddie accompany a foursome that rides. Many of the golf associations have created caddie scholarship funds by which thousands of outstanding club caddies with good grades in school have been awarded grants for colleges. Among the more renowned are the Western Golf Association's Chick Evans Scholarship Fund and the Long Island Caddie Scholarship Fund.

In the mid-1970s, the women's movement made its impact on the trade as clubs regularly began allowing females to caddie. Normally they would be assigned the lighter golf bags, and only rarely would they be expected to carry doubles (two bags) for 18-holes. Female caddies, usually pulling trolleys, are now the rule in Japan and throughout Asia. And there are even a few women caddying full-time on the PGA and LPGA Tours.

All told, the future of caddying is a mixed one. In North America, the caddie ranks have already suffered and are likely to shrink only gradually into the next century. Where the cart hasn't already decimated the ranks, many clubs are nervous about having the kinds of people hanging around their grounds who gravitate toward caddying. And there are additional considerations these days having to do with legal liability, unemployment insurance and workmen's compensation that create further obstacles for clubs trying to bring back caddies.

Course design has also had an effect. A boom in golf course construction in the late-1980s was oriented toward real estate development and residential players, with courses built exclusively for carts, and the holes spread out so far that caddies are effectively rendered obsolete by them. In the 1990s, golf course development has been driven by budgetary considerations that work against caddies. Clubs need to maximize (cart) revenues, while golfers who play daily-fee facilities are often reluctant to shell out the $30-35 caddie fee that has become standard. The best hope for caddies might well reside in the ultra-exclusive private clubs, like The Medalist in Hobe Sound, Florida or San Francisco Golf Club, where a certain traditionalism dictates form.

Worldwide, the prospects are somewhat better, for in many areas carts have not colonized the game and labor pools remain abundant. Here there is good reason for believing—and hoping—that over the coming decades, caddies will remain a crucial, though secondary, part of the game.

If the club caddie is waning, the caddies on the professional tournament circuit have never been stronger in their presence. No one knows the first time a player came from out of town and brought along his regular caddie. But we know something about those men who chose to make a life caddying on the tournament circuit. Around the time of World War I in the metropolitan New York City area, for instance, there emerged a flourishing golf circuit, both amateur and professional. A number of the local club caddies began traveling from site to site looking for upscale employment. The most famous of these was Joe Horgan, who taught Sarazen the caddie ropes. They apparently manifested such a highbrow moral demeanor that however foppish the low-budget lifestyle they lived, in Sarazen's words "all we ever stole was sleep."

The national tournament circuit was just getting under way, and the purses were so small that the players, let alone any caddies, could scarcely carve out a living. But if tournament work were conjoined with club caddying and all manner of small jobs here and there off-season, then it was worthwhile to spend some time caddying for the big boys. Joe Horgan, for instance, became Walter Hagen's regular caddie in the northeast tournament circuit. Overseas, Skip Daniels was much in demand, and at a considerable salary; in 1928, some 35 pounds for the week, far more than double the average workman's wage.

Tournament caddies have never been more valuable. Indeed, players now take their caddies overseas with them. For decades, for instance, American players going to Britain would make regular arrangements with caddies over there; the Englishman Cecil Timms was the regular choice in the early 1950s, and he won with Hogan at Carnoustie in 1953. In the 1960s Tip Anderson worked regularly for Arnold Palmer, and the late Alfie Fyles won five British Opens at Tom Watson's side.

Starting in 1974, the caddie trade became internationalized when Gary Player brought his regular American tour caddie, "Rabbit" Dyer, to work for him at Royal Lytham and St. Annes. Soon many top tour players followed, though often it was the caddie who paid the airfare. So large have tour purses become—and so inexpensive are standby international rates—that many caddies now make their own arrangements to work for players abroad. The first such bag-toting entrepreneur was Ernest "Creamy" Caroline, the elderly former band singer and one-time caddie for Arnold Palmer who is now the stuff of caddie lore. He first flew over for the British Open in 1976—in his mid-60s. Quite a number followed him, and it is now standard for most of the American golfers at a British Open to show up, caddie in tow. In 1979, the Europeans caught on when their Ryder Cup team flew its caddies over for the matches in the States. The trend has continued apace, and when Nick Faldo tees up in America—or anywhere in the world, for that matter—his regular caddie, Fanny Sunesson, is always on the bag.

So sophisticated have tour caddies become that in the U.S. they have formed the Professional Tour Caddie's Association. The nearly 125 members have negotiated several sponsorship contracts with companies whose apparel they wear. They even have their own little motor home, replete with a kitchen that supplies some of the best, and affordable, cuisine on site. Players regularly lunch there. The PTCA also monitors its membership for any unsavory behavior, and the effect has been to help raise considerably the social status of the tour caddies, to the point where they have good working relationships with tourna-

ı officials and local club representatives. They are also able
ɔɔ .rrange for discounted hotel accommodations and low-fare
flights to the next tournament site.

Unfortunately for the game, fewer and fewer of today's tour
caddies resemble the classical old characters who have
spawned so many golf stories. Overall, the caddies are younger
and more sober than two or three decades ago. A few of the old
guard are on the Seniors tour, but most of them have simply
not been able to compete in an era when instead of carpooling
from one tour site to the next, the caddies are regularly flying
and manage their own affairs with the help of briefcases, lap-
tops, and cellular phones.

With purses now topping a million dollars for a tournament, probably one-third of the 150 or so regular American
Tour caddies and about half as many on the European Tour are
actually able to bank some cash, or to use their earnings one
week for a vacation the next. Wages are the best-kept secret in
the trade, but by late 1996 the standard salary was $550 per
week plus 5 percent of earnings. Not bad, perhaps, if you caddie for Phil Mickelson when he's got $1.57 million by October.
But move down the money list somewhat and there's Donnie
Hammond struggling along at $90,813 for the year. At stan-
dard wages, that doesn't allow Hammond's caddie enough to
cover travel expenses. But some caddies have better financial
deals worked out and are hitched to more promising players.

What does a tour caddie actually do? On practice days he
walks the course, checking for lines of play and potential trouble spots. From the tee he selects an "aim point," particularly
on a dogleg, and then he walks out onto the fairway while taking note of lateral hazards, trees, and the lie of the rough. At
the preferred landing areas he then turns around and looks
back at the tee to see whether he's missed anything important.
Acquiring and checking proper yardage is not the art form it
used to be. All of the caddies now rely upon printed little
yardage books that detail distances on each hole. This has
taken good old guesswork out of the game and replaced it with
high-tech science. Indeed, the most recent "must-have" device
on Tour is an optical range finder, accurate to within 1/1,000th
of a yard. Technically, it violates Rule 14-3 and so can't be used

during tournament rounds. It's a great help during practice rounds, even if at $3,000 it's a tad pricey. But then, the cost of a single "bad yardage" could be even greater.

A professional player's golf bag is his mobile field office. The caddie's job is to make sure that all the equipment is in functioning order. Sufficient supplies of golf balls, tees, and gloves are indispensable. The rain gear has to be aboard, that extra sweater and another dry towel properly stowed away as well. Band-Aids, skin cream, whatever the player might need; all of it has to be available. For four hours the caddie will serve as the player's secretary, gofer, and janitor.

But if this were all that a caddie did, the job would be rather simple. One other precious piece of equipment has to be tended to: the most fragile component of the game. The player's ego is at center stage. It has to be stroked. The mind game has to be cared for. If fears are not subdued and the player's concentration not heightened, the best swing in the world will nonetheless collapse under the burdens of tournament pressure.

At the 1981 World Series of Golf at Firestone GC, I was able to line up a job with a young German making his American Tour debut—a fellow by the name of Bernhard Langer. Complex negotiations with his agent at the sports management firm IMG were aided by my ability to speak German. What I hadn't counted on was having to caddie in meters, not yards. The night after our first practice session I had created a conversion table based upon a 10 percent adjustment, whereby 100 yards equaled 90 meters. Langer, being precise to the extreme, corrected me the next morning. "Not ten percent," he reminded me. "Nine."

What a thrill, though, to be paired with the likes of Greg Norman and Tom Kite, and to make it on national TV, where my parents and friends could catch some "tube time" of me. The outfits we wore had the name of our player stitched above a flag denoting their country of origin. As we walked together toward the seventh green on Saturday, Kite asked if it bothered me as an American to have a German flag on my back? "What, are you kidding?" I answered, "I'm Jewish, and I'm not in the least bothered by the German flag. The only thing that counts is if this guy can shoot under par."

Langer played extremely well, and found himself on Sunday morning only two shots out. On the second hole, a modest par-five, he dumped his tee shot into a fairway bunker and had to bail out short. Then, from 147 yards away he flew a seven-iron into the cup for an eagle 3. Walking down the third fairway, we were now a shot clear of the field and I was so excited I began calculating my percentage check of the $100,000 first prize. I was shaking like a leaf.

The idea during a round is to inculcate positive thoughts in the player's mind as he approaches his next shot. But goodness knows, this can be difficult. As he made the turn for the final nine that Sunday, Langer was right in the middle of a dogfight and I was on shaky ground—and my nervousness was showing. Big mistake. For three days, everything came naturally. Now it became difficult to get the right yardage without betraying some excitement. Somewhere around the 12th hole his game began to unravel and I simply didn't know what to say or do. Not that anything would have helped, but this was a level of competitive pressure that was new to me. He made four bogies over the closing six holes and ended up tied for sixth place. Each bogey cost me a fortune. Within a few hours he had gone from $100,000 to $16,000, and my share shrank accordingly. I learned, then, how important it is to remain calm. Experienced caddies, like veteran players, are able to rise above the heat of the moment and not fall sway to their emotions.

There are times when things are going so badly that your golfer can hear the grass talking back at him. At other times, the caddie senses when a few words can turn the player's attention from his last shot to the next. Whatever the propriety of the moment, to speak up or to remain silent, the fundamental rule of caddying, the one that governs the entire relationship in the middle of a tournament round, is never to implant a bad idea or to suggest the possibility of failure. Don Pooley offered me some sound advice during a practice round at the 1978 PGA at Oakmont. Having surveyed all the danger spots on the course, we then sat down for our (his) final strategy session. He told me never to mention things that might go wrong. "It's all very simple," he said. "No negative thoughts."

By social class and upbringing, the caddie is a marginal outsider. But by virtue of a peculiarly cultivated knowledge, he finds himself very much on the inside. Thus the caddie suffers a strange and alienating fate. He is the outsider as insider. He makes the smallest of differences to the well-being of his player, perhaps a shot or two per week, and from this difference he draws a living. The player will go on to fame and riches. The caddie, by contrast, will be left behind.

Though perhaps even that is changing. After winning the 1992 PGA championship at Bellerive CC near St. Louis, Nick Price had to wait outside the media tent before giving his interview. It seems his caddie, Jeff ("Squeaky") Medlin, was inside doing his own press conference. Having also won the PGA the year before with John Daly, "Squeaky" had become something of a star in his own right. A few years later when he became ill with leukemia, the news made headlines.

So, too, did word of Mike "Fluff" Cowan having switched from Peter Jacobsen to Tiger Woods. This was, after all, a veteran caddie who had already appeared in ESPN ads, including one promo for the Las Vegas Invitational in which he was dressed up in an Elvis outfit. By the time his man won the golf tournament in October 1996, both player and caddie had become celebrities.

Stand by Your Woman

Shelley Hamlin, a longtime LPGA Tour veteran, was having a tough season. All year she had won only a few thousand dollars, and now, as I caddied for her at St. George's Golf & Country Club in Toronto for the 1984 duMaurier Classic, she was suffering through a difficult second round. She had started the day with a fair chance to make the 36-hole cut, but after a poor front nine she scraped the ball around on the par-three 13th hole for an ungainly double-bogie. Her tee shot on the 14th was equally uninspired, and as she trudged down the fairway she turned to me and moaned, "I'm so depressed."

A smile slowly lit up my face. Unexpectedly, her words resolved an issue that had plagued me the whole week, my first as a caddie on the ladies' Tour. Until her utterance I could not understand the attraction of caddying for the women. But right there on the 14th fairway the mystery was solved. Simply stated, the women play their game on a human scale, and though they do so exceptionally well, they are also not afraid to express their emotions.

The distinct attraction of women's professional golf is that these distaffers do not let the allure of fame and fortune stifle their feelings as they play. And no one sees this from a better vantage point than the Tour caddie. As bag-toter and personal confidant, you are out there between the ropes with the privilege and responsibility to stand by your woman.

Back in the mid-1960s, Dee Darden was flying Air Force fighter planes and photo-reconnaissance missions. Two decades later his feet were planted firmly on the ground as Nancy Lopez's regular caddie during some of her prime golfing days. After retiring from the service in 1976 with the rank of Lieutenant Colonel, he prepared to work for a civilian airline ambulance service in the state of Washington. But some of his golfing friends suggested he spend a few weeks caddying on the PGA Tour. After a few East Coast events he headed back home, and while driving through Springfield, Illinois, stopped off at the Jerry Lewis Muscular Dystrophy Classic to earn himself some gas money.

It turned out to be a major LPGA event, and he found that even with all the big-name players there, the tournament exuded an intimacy not found on the men's Tour. Over the next month he encountered the same atmosphere at other LPGA events. And so he decided to put aside his flying career and travel around the country with the women's Tour.

The path to the LPGA caddie ranks has many routes. Augie Gramf, who toted many years for Jane Blalock, took early retirement as a New York City detective in order to come out. Jean Darden, Dee's wife, had ambitions to turn pro and decided to inspect the competition firsthand. What she found out in 1979 was a level of play somewhat beyond her own, and she learned so much by watching the game up close that she decided to shift careers and concentrate upon caddying.

About 80 percent of the 144 golfers in each LPGA event bring along their own caddies. Most of them are regulars, others are culled from that floating crew of ex-real estate brokers, college graduates, short-order cooks and former country club loopers looking for a change of pace who do not (yet) have steady work.

There are three sorts of "open" players. Some simply do not believe in relying upon a single caddie and prefer to play the market. Others, usually the veterans, rely upon ad hoc arrangements with a few select caddies whom they know well. Players from both groups usually line up a caddie weeks in advance or show up at the course on Tuesday morning to pick up a regular Tour caddie who is free that week. A third group, perhaps 10 percent of all the LPGA players, are on a tight budget and prefer to save money by hiring a local caddie at what are invariably bargain rates.

The women professionals tend to stay looser than their male counterparts in actual competition. Instead of displaying an unrelenting drive and intensity, they practice what might be termed "selective concentration." It isn't that they're not being serious so much as that their seriousness turns on and off for each shot.

A large part of the caddie's job is to allow for this selective concentration. To keep things relaxed between shots the player and caddie will revert to a lighthearted banter that, to a casual observer behind the ropes, might sound like mindless chatter. "We would talk all the time between shots," says Dee Darden, "about music, parties, places to eat and about her baby, Ashley." Those who try to emulate Ben Hogan by concentrating intently without interruption are likely to find themselves driven off the Tour with a bad case of the nerves.

No negative thoughts, only positive ones. When you stand over the ball preparing to play away there is no room for doubt or anxiety. A caddie doesn't say "Watch out for the water;" he says "Carry it to the center of the green." If the player pulls out a club from the bag that the caddie believes is the wrong one, he doesn't try to talk her out of it. This is a fundamental rule of caddying; never take a club out of the player's hand, so to speak, unless asked. If she asks, "Four- or five-iron?" then you tell her. But if she pulls out the five-iron and says nothing, stand back, pray for a little wind and hope she makes a full swing. After the round you can express your doubts, but a tournament round is not the occasion for such criticism. It is, rather, the time when a player needs assurance from her junior partner.

Thus the LPGA Tour caddies are more than bag-toters and golf advisors. They are ego boosters, therapists of sort, raconteurs, and part-time companions. A few have also wound up marrying—or in some cases, divorcing—the women for whom they went to work.

The public rewards heaped upon a successful player only indirectly filter down to her caddie. There is a shared, but unequal responsibility for the golf shots played under pressure. Yet in their modest way, the caddies do make those shots a little easier to play, and the small percentage of bonus they receive in return properly reflects their contribution.

There are, however, smaller rewards to caddying, less tangible if no less satisfying. When Shelley Hamlin approached her ball that day in the rough alongside the 14th fairway, she found it only a few inches from the spot where she had dumped her four-iron shot into the creek fronting the green the previous day. The ball had not jumped yesterday from the flyer lie. So we stood there thinking about the shot, the same playing conditions as yesterday, and the yardage to the pin, which was about the same. She looked at me, grimaced, and without saying what she was thinking communicated her thoughts clearly enough. I assured her the four-iron was indeed the correct club, and that those who preside over this strange game had visited upon her a chance to make amends. She nodded silently, addressed the ball with confidence, and made a very solid swing. The ball took off on just the right trajectory, straight at the pin. It came to a halt just a few feet short of the hole. Shelley turned to me and brightened. "That was much better," she said. "More of those and I wouldn't be so depressed."

∽

The '96 Mid-Am: A View
from the Caddie Yard

Imagine having a major golf tournament in your own back yard! That was the beauty of the 1996 USGA Mid-Am. The sixteenth running of this tournament for the 30-something crowd was being held just a few miles from my house, and on two courses I regularly play. Tumble Brook CC, in my town of Bloomfield, CT, was to host one of the stroke play rounds. Just down the road lies Hartford GC, the site of the other stroke play round, and then four grueling days of match play.

Earlier in the week I made two phone calls in hopes of finding a loop. The first went to Vinny Giles, a Virginia native whose substantial claims to fame include the 1972 U.S. Amateur title, four Walker Cup teams (1969/71/73/75), a win at the 1975 British Amateur, and low amateur in the '96 British Senior Open. The other call went to Jim Stahl, a businessman from Cincinnati, Ohio, who had won the '95 Senior Amateur and then suffered the humiliation at the '96 Senior Open of being paired with Tom Weiskopf. As everyone now knows, Weiskopf withered Stahl with all sorts of steamy and insulting rhetoric, for which Weiskopf has apologized (sort of), including a brief, indirect letter to Stahl—which Weiskopf's secretary signed. Stahl, meanwhile, received over 200 letters of support, including a dozen from PGA Tour pros.

Giles returned my call first, and so we agreed I'd caddie for him. Golf being a game of great ironies, we were paired the first day of practice with the man everybody here endearingly calls "Grandpa," the 57-year old Stahl.

There are all sorts of players in this field in terms of age, weight, body type, social class, and golf experience. That's the beauty of truly open events like this one, especially with the enlarged field of 264 (only the U.S. Amateur is larger: 312). Unlike single-course events like the U.S. Open where the field has to be limited to 156 players, the Mid-Am draws upon two neighboring golf courses and thus, despite the early fall slot on the calendar (i.e., only 12 hours of daylight), can still get in the big group.

Many of the players know each other because so many are regulars in local and national events. About a third carry their own light golf bags. A few have their wives, girlfriends, buddies, or a family member toting. And the demands of caddying are not quite as extreme as on the PGA Tour. For example, the competitors rely upon marked sprinkler yardage to the centers of the greens and then adjust accordingly for the pins. The USGA acquiesces in this by making pin sheets available to competitors each morning. These have the green depths and then indicate how far into each green that day's pin is. It makes for easy calculations and helps ease the pace of play. USGA officials figure that at 4:20 per round, they can finish; at 4:30 they'll run into darkness.

The first day Giles played Tumble Brook. It's an older style layout, well manicured, with holes incorporating three different eras. What a shame that six inches of rain had fallen in the past three weeks. The grounds were soaked. What made matters worse was that the unseasonably cool air was also heavy with humidity. Result? The ball goes nowhere. Add to that the effects of a 25-30 mph wind and some holes were nearly unreachable. Most of the field hit full middle-irons for their third shots into the upwind 562-yard par-five 17th hole. Even downwind holes played long, like the 507-yard par-five 5th hole, which was just beyond the reach of two full-bore woods by Giles.

For the record, he shot a three-over par 75. Pretty fair, except that he hit 14 greens in regulation and used up 34 putts along the way. Don't blame me. I gave perfect yardage, and we conferred and agreed on every iron club and on every read of the greens. It was just difficult making putts. Jim Stahl, meanwhile, who on a calm day doesn't drive the ball 220 yards, was low man at Tumble Brook with a one-under 71. The cut for advancing to match play looked like six-over par 149.

Sunday, round two of stroke-play qualifying for match play, the weather was clear and the wind down—this after another inch of rain further saturated the golf course. I swear, for Sunday's round, there were three tees that could have played as casual water.

Amazing how easy caddying is when your man is under par. My man Giles played like a genius and once again did not putt really well. Thirteen greens hit in regulation and he winds up at 70, one-under par, at Hartford GC. He took 31 putts, three fewer than the first day, but that's largely because he holed out a 65-yard wedge for eagle 3 on the par-five ninth hole. All told, he missed five birdie putts inside 10 feet and bogeyed the last two holes, both from the bunker. One of those 70s that could have been a 65 real easy. We got along fine out there, discussing every club, and my reading all his first putts. Reading wasn't the problem, though; stroking it correctly was. But the main thing was that he's made it to the round of 64 for matches. His 145 total, two-over-par, was only six shots off the medalist's score of 139 and placed him in the fifteenth seed.

Few people could have been hitting the ball better over two days of qualifying than my man Vinny. He had hit 27 greens in regulation and 19 of 27 fairways. But the flat stick was still something of a sore spot. So going into match play there was reason to be concerned. Also to be anxious, since by prior agreement I would not be able to caddie for him, owing to a teaching commitment that I could not get out of. The plan, then, was for me to hand over responsibility for the day to a very reliable caddie and then to pick up Giles' bag again on Tuesday if—if—he made it through.

What a helpless feeling. His match went off at 2 p.m., and there I was teaching and then driving home and I couldn't think about anything all day but the match. By the time I could get back to the golf course at 6:30, the result would be in.

I rehearsed several different responses, and could only construct an imaginary match in my mind.

The opponent in the first of six match-play rounds was Frank Ford III, a Charleston, South Carolina stockbroker. One of the compelling aspects of the Mid-Am is that the field very much treats the tournament like a reunion. Most of the players are veterans of the amateur circuit, and for someone like Giles, with 30 years of nationally-ranked and world-class experience behind him, there are few good players he hasn't already seen, especially when they hail from the south. Giles, who lives in Richmond, Virginia, plays loads of golf up and down the southeast coast. He was also paired with Ford in practice rounds. I replayed all the shots of theirs I could remember to see who might have had an advantage. The odds, I kept reminding myself, were 50:50 no matter what.

I raced back to Hartford GC. There was Giles' car still in the lot. A good sign? I couldn't tell. I breathlessly headed over to the grill and there in a corner sat Vinny Giles with his caddie and some local friends. Empty cups were scattered on the table and they were obviously working on a follow-up round.

I looked at them; they looked at me. No indication.

Then he said it. "Well, caddie, I guess you let me down. Guess I couldn't do it without you. 'Course the way I putted, I couldn't have done it with you, either."

What is it they say about golfers who reach a certain age—that the first thing to go is their putting? Actually, it turns out the ball striking wasn't quite as sharp either. Giles, normally a brilliant wedge player, twice laid the sod over the ball from inside 60 yards. Worse yet, he jacked two uphill putts inside three feet that would have narrowed the deficit to two-down. Ford, meanwhile, was dive-bombing putts in that, had they missed, would have ended up yards away. It was over at the 14th green, 5 and 4.

For all but a handful of competitors in the Mid-Am, the goal is to make it to match play. Two days of medal play tells you how well you're playing. From there in, match play is something of a matter of luck. Only the very strongest of players can really expect to march through their brackets, and while there's no solace to be taken in losing, there's much to be said for being among the elite 64 who make it that far while thousands of others who tried to, could not.

During our medal play rounds we were paired with a young man whose attitude grew more sullen and petulant as his scores went ever higher. One thing I've learned as a 13 handi-capper is that it's not how well you play but how well you han-dle how you play. And so our young companion withered into realms of public self-reproach, at one point early on the final nine inquiring about "the last flight outta here" and another time saying something about "Oh well, maybe I can go home and play in some handicap events." He carried his own bag and so, lacking the proverbial whipping post, relied upon me as a sounding board. But I refused to give him the comfort he so desperately craved. Finally, I could take no more, and at the 15th green, as he wailed again, I simply said that "I'm honored just to take part in this as a caddie. I would think anyone would be proud to be playing in it." There was no claim of moral high ground here; just a modest attempt at invoking an ethic of the game.

3

A Writer's Game

Caddying for Pat Ward-Thomas
at the Old Course

A Moslem must go at least once in his lifetime to Mecca. For a Jew, a pilgrimage to the Wailing Wall in Jerusalem is no less obligatory. The golfer? His grail is a voyage to the promised land of Scotland, where golf as we know it took form and where writers about this humbling game can revive their spirits.

Some years ago I took a working holiday to Scotland. My plan: to caddie my way through Scotland, playing as many of the fabled courses as possible. Predictably, I suppose, I preferred playing to caddying, but after rounds at Muirfield and North Berwick, I sensed the need to generate more income.

Where better than on the far side of the Firth of Forth, and a few miles farther north and east, at the Old Course at St. Andrews? It seemed a good time and place to begin, and it promised to be lucrative, a single bag reaping 10 pounds (about $20 or so back then) for a round.

I arrived at St. Andrews in September of 1980, in time for the Royal and Ancient Golf Club's Autumn Medal, its annual club matches. While this restricted the available starting times, it held the promised of regular employment. I arranged for a bed and breakfast within walking distance of the Old Course—indeed, almost everything in this medieval town is little more than a par-five away from the starter's box—and headed for the course.

Most golfers recognize that imposing stone edifice, the clubhouse of the Royal and Ancient Golf Club. It presides over the Old Course like a temple in golf's holy land. More interesting to me, however, was the modest wood-frame cottage just before the clubhouse, behind the 18th green. Here, sharing quarters with the golf shop, was the caddiemaster's office.

I was dressed a tad shabbily for a tourist, yet far too neatly for a caddie. I persuaded the somewhat incredulous Angus (all caddiemasters seem to lack a last name) that I wanted to work, and that my experience on the PGA Tour and at U.S. clubs gave me credentials for this most august of bag-toting responsibilities. He relented and told me to return in the morning. "There might be work," he grumbled.

As a newcomer to this last local guild of craftsmen, I was the final caddie to be used. I was called regularly, however; although never before 11 a.m. Rather than squander the morning—as if there were anything else to do in town—I would arrive with my golf clubs just before sunrise, tee off well before the first official starting time, and saunter up the 18th fairway by about 9:30 a.m., with a day's round already behind me. In this manner, I played and caddied the Old Course every day for a month.

I never broke 90, yet I always seemed to play the final hole decently. Nothing is more satisfying than to hit a tee shot beyond Granny Clark's Wynd, the path crossing the final fairway, then loft a short iron or run a wee pitch shot through the Valley of Sin (a depression fronting the 18th green) within birdie range. If you do this, you're able, somehow, to convince yourself that the putt doesn't matter.

In any event, my first two rounds on the Old Course ended with glorious pars, and though I said nothing, I suspected this accorded me a measure of credibility in the eyes of Angus. After all, he had only to look out his office window to the last hole. What did he know of my earlier travails on the far end of the golf course?

While I could not affect the accent of a gnarled, white-haired, chain-smoking caddie, I could acquire a knowledge of the Old Course, such as the names of the bunkers (Kruger, Mrs. Kruger, Strath, Beardies, Hell, Scholars, and of course, The Principal's Nose). And I could learn how, despite the apparent openness of the left side of each driving area, the par-fours are best reached down the right side.

After a few days of caddying for tourists, I spotted the name of Pat Ward-Thomas on the starter's sheet. For years the golf correspondent of *The Guardian*, he had also written for the magazine *Country Life*, succeeding Bernard Darwin, perhaps the greatest of all golf writers. Ward-Thomas had been pouring out a stream of columns and books on golf and was famous throughout Britain, or so I thought. And now I, an American, had the temerity to think I might caddie for him at the Old Course?

An idea came to me. A true golfer would stay at one of only a few hotels in St. Andrews. It shouldn't be too much of a task to find his. I tried Rusack's, which overlooks the 18th fairway, but as soon as I walked in I realized that golf writer's couldn't make *this* much money. No, he wasn't there. I surveyed the other first-class inns. Just behind the R&A clubhouse, down the shoreline road east of the golf course, was a hostelry where he was scheduled to arrive that evening. I left a brief note: If he weren't committed to another caddie, I would gladly work for him the next day. I added that I admired his writing.

The next morning, Angus noted with mild puzzlement that I was dressed more upscale than usual: corduroy jacket, a tie under my pullover sweater, and walking shoes rather than sneakers. I retired to the far end of the bench and stared at the morning newspaper, scarcely able to read a paragraph.

Thoughts about the day ambled through my head. With an obsessiveness that I was convinced was really appropriate caution, I studied each golfer who approached the caddie shack to see if any fit my image of what an esteemed, elderly golf writer should look like. It was a teasingly pleasurable mind game.

The morning passed slowly. Fifteen minutes before Ward-Thomas' starting time, I concluded he would not ask for me, thereby dealing a fatal blow to the career of a promising golf writer: Ignored by a worldly scribe, all alone in Scotland, money running out, suddenly unsure whether my parents *really* loved me, now dismissed as insignificant by the lordly Pat Ward-Thomas. How quickly one's world unravels.

A frail man appeared out of nowhere. He was no more than 5-foot-7, perhaps 130 pounds, dressed in dullish beige and wearing rubber-soled deck shoes rather than standard golf footwear. Beneath his gray hair was a face etched by what must have been a millennium of howling winds. He paused at the caddiemaster's Dutch door to light a filterless cigarette, then leaned through the upper half of the door to say something to Angus. He unfurled the piece of paper I had left at the hotel and showed it to the caddiemaster.

Angus nodded, then walked slowly over to me and said, "Go with this man." Feigning casualness, I arose, picked up a small golf bag by the fence, and then introduced myself quickly to Ward-Thomas. No great need for conversation, here, I figured. I would save it for the round.

I prepared to hand him his driver at the first tee, but I noticed something strange: an extra stiff shaft. It would take enormous hand strength to use such a club. Ward-Thomas came over to me as I tested the flex of this super-club.

"A personal gift from Arnold Palmer," he gloated.

Perhaps writers are by nature immodest. It takes courage to go public all the time. In any case, this writer insisted on waiting for the foursome ahead to cross Swilcan Burn fronting the first green before he would hit his tee shot.

Ward-Thomas fidgeted. He shifted and reshifted his paltry weight. Finally, he lashed the club with the fury of a scorned god. A massive divot flew through the air. The ball dribbled a few pathetic yards before coming to rest under the white fence to the right of the fairway. This was only the beginning.

Ward-Thomas played horribly, perhaps the worst I have ever witnessed. At one time or another, his club must have struck the ball at every conceivable angle. An iron shot not topped or shanked would almost certainly be duck-hooked. What passed for a short game rarely succeeded in delivering the ball halfway to the hole. And for his touch on the greens, it was, let us say, somewhat defensive.

"I haven't putted past the hole since 1948," he glowered on the fourth green, after leaving yet another putt short.

He was not playing as well as he (presumably) could. In fact, he probably never had. It mattered little, though, because throughout the round there gushed forth from him the most extraordinary cascade of profanity, deserved self-reproaches, and condemnations of the game's very existence.

I shall never forget how, in the stillness of a perfect, sky-blue autumn afternoon, he dumped his second shot into Strath bunker at the short 11th hole. He looked about forlornly for a moment, then slowly looked up, up into the sky, and raised his arms against it in anguished protest. There, several miles above, was the thin condensation trail of an airplane. Ward-Thomas, outraged, railed furiously at the apparent cause of his latest golf misfortune.

"Flaming Royal Air Force ought to be disbanded," he screamed.

On and on he went—the violent force, the eruptive nature of his words. They seemed to emanate from some deep inner core of horror, from a profound knowledge—never to be admitted—that he could not play this game on a level at which he knew it must be played.

Yet his self-abuse was endearing. Along with his oral transgressions against the whole existence of humanity there developed between us a discourse about the merits of the Old Course's design. This aging man (then 67), obviously unhealthy, slashed his way across the sacred land he knew so well, puffing on cigarettes between each foozled shot, taking the time between crescendos of expletives to analyze the mysteries of St. Andrews. He would point out subtleties of the course that alone I would never have perceived. I began to think that gnomes, working furtively at night, were altering the terrain I had come to know. Could it be that Pat Ward-Thomas was privy to their nocturnal genius? Or perhaps they were carrying out a master plan that he had secretly devised.

Whatever the case, he knew more about the Old Course than it is bearable to know. Yet, to suffer the ignominy of playing so terribly upon it is a refined form of golf torture—to be so intimate with a game that he played so poorly.

After the round he paid me, sparingly. He told me that he was off to Ireland to review some newly opened golf course for a magazine.

Trudging back to my bed and breakfast, I pondered the experience. I envied the ability of that man to profit elegantly from the vice of his addiction. I also thought it a worthy life to earn one's living writing about something you knew so much about, yet something at which you could never do well enough yourself.

Pat Ward-Thomas died two years later. I later found out he

had been a much better player, and I had caught him during the down phase of his golfing skills. I doubt, however, my experience with him would have been half as interesting had he played well.

CO

A Thousand Words to Clear His Throat: Herbert Warren Wind

Former USGA Executive Director Frank Hannigan once said that he never read a description of a golf hole that did it any justice. The best architecture writing is not about what this or that hole looks like. Rather, it is about what it feels like to be on a particular golf course and to sense and feel the beauty of tradition that distinguishes one memorable layout from another. Bernard Darwin's classic study, *The Golf Courses of the British Isles* (1910), does just that. So, too, did Pat Ward-Thomas' work for *Country Life*.

Golf course journalism today tends to suffer from a number of constraints. The first is of space. Most editors do not allow their writers the column inches enjoyed by writers of an earlier era, so it is hard even to get going in terms of style and argument. The focus today also tends to be narrower. The modern emphasis is on hyperbole: best, greatest, toughest. Subtlety is sacrificed, in terms both of course criticism and ultimately, of course design.

Among the precious few holdovers from an earlier school of golf course writing is Herbert Warren Wind, longtime sportswriter for *The New Yorker*. Herb, as he invites you to call him, is the dean of postwar golf writers. Today, he is retired and lives outside of Boston, 20 miles north of the working class town of Brockton where he was born in 1917. For years, he usually wrote just a few long articles a year, essays filled with the history of course architecture, with the great players of yesteryear, with the evolution of the game, and with the sportsmanship it cultivates. His essays invariably followed the Masters and the U.S. Open by some six weeks. It seemed as if the tournament was not really over until Herb's article had appeared.

He once said it took him about 1,000 words to clear his throat. Perhaps that's why he left *Sports Illustrated* in 1961 after having helped start the magazine. He went back to *The New Yorker*, then on to the television production of "Shell's Wonderful World of Golf."

That show opened up the eyes of a whole generation of golfers to the world's memorable courses. For an hour every Saturday afternoon, golf fans were transported to St. Andrews or Royal Melbourne for a world-class education. While ostensibly a means to bring together two international golf stars for match play, "Shell's Wonderful World of Golf" was unique in devoting attention to legendary venues.

Back then I did not know about Herbert Warren Wind. I only stumbled upon him by chance in 1966, when as a twelve-year-old I read and reread his two-part series in *Golf Digest* about the history of golf course architecture. New York-based course architect Stephen Kay later told me that reading those two articles changed his life and made him determined to go into course design. The effect on me was similar. I was especially struck by the quirky characters whom Wind profiled: Charles Blair Macdonald, Alister MacKenzie, A.W. Tillinghast, Donald Ross. I have since been unable to get these rogues out of my study.

Years later I finally met Herb. It was the 1979 U.S. Open at Inverness Club in Toledo, Ohio, and I was spending the summer caddying on the PGA Tour. I had just read the third edition of *The Story of American Golf*, and when I got to Inverness I decided to try to say hello to Mr. Wind. So I wrote him a long fawning letter and brought it over sheepishly to the press tent security guard with instructions to pass it on.

The next day I returned and asked for a Mr. Herbert Warren Wind. The guard disappeared into the tent. I fidgeted for a few minutes, and then out came this British-looking gentleman, a character out of a P.G. Wodehouse story. He was gracious and thoughtful, and after we had talked briefly, he encouraged me to stay in contact with him.

Many of Herb's golf articles from *The New Yorker* were gathered together in *Following Through* (1986). He also contributed regularly on tennis, as well as the occasional odd piece. My favorite nongolf essay of his is a 70-page history of field-goal kicking. The article moves painstakingly through each decade of American football, documenting how changes in both the shape of the ball and in kicking techniques affected this singular method of scoring. About halfway through the article, I began to get depressed over the realization that the article was eventually going to end.

I had the pleasure of accompanying Herb during the final round of the 1982 U.S. Open at Pebble Beach. The day was moderately warm, but Wind came to the course prepared for the worst possible weather. He wore a tweed suit and a smart-looking little cap and carried a raincoat (with wool liner) on one arm. His feet were protected by insulated walking shoes. What could he possibly wear in wintertime? Around his neck was a pair of opera glasses, and he also carried a little note pad in which he scribbled throughout the round. One of his free hands clasped an umbrella, which doubled as a walking stick.

Wind is a traditionalist. As we stood around the third green, one of the new breed of golf fans excitedly informed us that "Bill Rogers was making only 19 percent of his birdie putts that week." Herb thanked him for this invaluable information, and as we walked off to the fourth tee turned to me and asked "What in the word does that have to do with golf?"

Jack Nicklaus was at this point in the midst of a fabulous birdie run, and so we walked on ahead to catch him. Then we held back and waited for Tom Watson and followed him in from the 12th. We stood there at the tee on the par-three 17th and watched Tom bury his tee shot into the rough left of the putting surface. Then we walked up and stood before the entrance to the green as Watson deftly chipped his way into the record books. As the ball plunked into the hole, it seemed the whole world around us exploded with cheers. Herb threw his hands up in the air and looked as joyous as a child.

4

Architectural Elements

Architectural Literacy

A sensitivity toward golf course architecture is essential to appreciating the game. Yet a variety of factors, ranging from media coverage of the game to an increasing reliance upon the golf cart, conspires to create a kind of public negligence when it comes to understanding golf courses. With all the congratulatory hoopla today about how popular golf is becoming and about how many new golf courses are needed for the coming decades, there is little concern that a significant component of the golfing public is architecturally illiterate.

No, this isn't a call for standardized tests and licenses for golfers. Nor is it the equally elitist claim that only a few cognoscenti really know the secrets of the game while the great unwashed masses languish in ignorance. Quite to the contrary, the great thing about golf is that it is so much fun and so humbling an experience regardless of your handicap or experience. But the more one pays attention to course design, the more one appreciates golf.

After all, the golf course is the least standardized playing field of any sport. Outside the diameter of the hole, everything is up for grabs: length and width of fairways, the size of tees and greens, numbers and shapes of bunkers, type and height of foliage. Yet, despite the lack of distinct rules, there are some basic principles of course design.

First of all, a golf course ought to look like it belongs there as part of the land. It should make good use of the terrain, wending its way through varied ground and routed so as to maximize, during the course of a round, a player's exposure to the winds and elements. Its greens ought to be well-sited, on natural plateaus and modest depressions, and the approach area to the greens ought to emphasize proper lines and angles of play from the fairways and tees. Its greens should be of varied size, not so large as to make the approach shot an indifferent matter but not so small and severe as to make it possible only for certain grades of players, say single-digit handicappers or professionals, to be able to play the course.

Demanding that the average golfer (and the average golfer, despite all manner of high-tech breakthroughs in golf still carries an 18-handicap) hit high fade irons and 220-yard tee shots across water hazards with no alternative path is not part of good architecture. There is no correlation between difficulty and quality. Such features only mislead players into thinking that golf was meant to be played one way. Instead, the golf course ought to encourage diverse shot making: playing modestly for sides of fairways; running up the approaches through the apron; learning the art of greenside chipping; and the kind of salvage game whereby one-putt pars or two-putt bogies become worthy pursuits. A well-designed golf course accommodates golfers of all skills.

You wouldn't know this today from television coverage. When most golfers experience Pebble Beach or Augusta National, they do so through the eyes of tournament players and through the analyses offered either by ex-players or those announcers whose basic function in life, it seems, is to celebrate the modern touring pro. Occasionally, there might be a mention that the course was designed by an A.W. Tillinghast or a Perry Maxwell, but beyond the passing reference there's never, ever, the slightest accounting of what such a classical pedigree entails. All we know from listening to such accounts and from tournament reporting in the next day's papers is that so and so hit a driver and five-iron to some 513 yard par-five.

Golf holes, accordingly, are rated for their "toughness" and for being "the hardest" and "the longest." But such claims lack any real meaning for most golfers, except that golfers then begin to think about their own course in the same terms as those used to judge what they've seen or read about on the tournament circuit.

From another perspective, golfers who take golf carts deny themselves full access to the architectural experience. They're moving too fast, they don't have a clear sense of the subtle angles of play to the green, and because they invariably approach the green from aside or behind, they rarely get a full sense of how the green's contours present themselves for play.

That's not to say that carts ought to be banned. Far from it, a lot of people are now able to enjoy golf who, before the advent of the golf cart, might not have been able to play at all. And other golfers, if they want to take a golf cart, well, that's their business. But they're missing out on something when they do. They're missing out on the aesthetics of the course, and they're helping undermine standards because as golf cart paths are built to accommodate them, golfers begin to see such features as normal. And when clubs require of all players that they ride, then they are denying golfers access to a subtler appreciation of course design.

The point, then, is that one should pay attention to the golf course, should walk as many good courses as possible, and demand of those who claim knowledge of the game that they tell us more about the elements of sound architecture. An intrepid few might even venture into those few available classic books of course design in the battle against architectural illiteracy and the quest for a more meaningful golf experience.

Classical, Modern, and Post-Modern

Golf course architecture is a creative endeavor. Its products can be understood as works of art. Players who focus only on the yardages to various points on the course or how to negotiate the hazards of a hole miss what good design is all about. The golf course is a product of three basic inputs: native land, human imagination, and technology. Regardless of how old or new a layout is, it can be assessed in terms of these three elements. Over time, it is possible to discern several basic styles of design that have resulted. Let us call them the classical, the modern, and the post-modern.

The first, the classical, derives from the origins of the game along the Scottish seacoast. The earliest golf courses emerged gradually along the receding linksland. No earth was moved, no plantings made. Players simply stroked the ball from one spot to the next. Eventually, paths of play developed, and then people assumed responsibility for maintaining the clearances that had evolved. Thus the origins of the greenkeeper. Sand bunkers were not built; they evolved where local golfers habitually gouged out the turf or where native animals, seeking shelter from the winds, had created sandy hollows.

At a certain point, generally around the middle of the nineteenth century, the old Scottish links were lengthened and updated for play to accommodate increased traffic. Still, the basic sites remained very much as men had originally found them. A few wheelbarrows of dirt were hauled from here to there, and some flattening and rolling of surfaces was needed to achieve appropriate teeing grounds and putting surfaces. But the game's tradition was to utilize available land and to run the holes through natural dunes and features.

All that changed around the turn of the century when golf moved south and inland to England. That is when golf course design proper developed as a craft. Site preparation became a subject of much study. Essays that began appearing before the First World War concerned themselves with preparing meadowland and parkland for golf's demands. Issues of drainage became paramount. Initially, surface water was steered into gullies, but it did not take long for subsurface pipe drainage to be added as well. Sand bunkers, originally an attempt to recapture the seaside feel of the classical links, were artificially installed. Hundreds of cubic yards of fill had to be moved to build the greens complexes and teeing areas.

This period, particularly in the 1920s, was golf design's most inventive era. Site selection was based upon the preexisting natural rolls and features of the land. Architects like Tillinghast, Ross, and MacKenzie were often free to choose one plot or the next down the road as they searched for more suitable land. Horse-drawn scrapers could shave off slices of land and make a few decisive cuts for the sake of visibility. But most of the work was done by hand; much of it, it must be admitted, by low-wage immigrant laborers. Earthmoving was limited to what could be dynamited and carted away.

The modern era began with the advent of major earthmoving equipment in the late 1920s/early 1930s. The steam shovel enabled architects to build up mounds in a matter of hours rather than days. The subsequent introduction of tractors and bulldozers gave architects a freedom that liberated them from the constraints of the site. This was the beginning of what came to be known as total site preparation: the use of automated equipment to plow down trees, level the earth, and create featuring entirely by machine. It soon became customary to move hundreds of thousands of cubic yards of dirt.

The modern look reached its pinnacle in the late 1950s/early 1960s, with the smooth clean look of Robert Trent Jones and those who followed in his trail, invariably with less talent and verve: Dick Wilson, George Cobb, Joe Lee, and Joe Finger. They emphasized massive scale and the power game. Classical design had rewarded shot making, maneuverability, and the ground game. Modern design, by contrast, emphasized high, lengthy shots.

In emulation of Augusta National, greens got enormous. Bunkers were built not so much to attract the eye as to facilitate cheap and easy maintenance. The cookie-cutter model of design was perfected by Geoffrey Cornish; his work, in particular, enabled thousands of public golfers to enjoy the game at low cost, but a price was paid in terms of creativity. It was the triumph of function over art form.

In its early days, modern golf design had liberated the game from natural constraints and had heralded an extraordinary improvement in course conditioning. But the work also became formulaic. Courses lost subtlety and their relationship with the land. The game became a kind of automatic enterprise, a characteristic confirmed with the introduction of motorized golf carts, which further removed players from the experience of terrain.

A few architects responded with a return to classical values. The first great counterrevolutionary blow was struck by Pete Dye at The Golf Club and then especially at Harbor Town; here, he and Jack Nicklaus suddenly returned the game to moderate scale: smaller greens, championship quality in 6,500 yards, and the inventive mounding and swales found in the classical seaside courses. Dye also evoked the earlier courses with his use of railroad ties—a common feature of Scottish courses, but unseen in the U.S. until the late 1960s.

The contemporary golf course has utilized contrivance in an attempt to emulate tradition. Now there are jagged boulders along the water's edge, vast stretches of unkempt wasteland, sharp edges between turf and desert, and steep bunkers of gothic proportion. The post-modern golf course fragments the natural unity of land. It utilizes technology and science to resurrect aspects of classical tradition. But it does so ironically, as if mocking that traditional look. At the same time, it recovers the environmental soundness of its classical predecessors.

The post-modern look championed by Dye has been taken in different directions, and with various degrees of success by (among others) Tom Fazio, Jay Morrish, and by some of Nicklaus' work in the desert. Robert Trent Jones, Jr. has taken the linear fairway and transformed it through vast three-dimensional motion. Rees Jones, by contrast, has relied, at times to excess, upon turtle-back mounding and counter-sloped containment lines to build golf courses fitted to the surrounds.

The beauty of a golf hole is that it has been, at least some extent, envisioned, planned, and engineered. Perhaps it was Nicklaus who once said that "90 percent of a golf course is below the surface," by which, of course, he meant irrigation, drainage and soil treatment, and layering. The ideal, of course, is that the contrivance of human intervention will lead to something that looks like it belongs there. In commenting upon the praise that a friend had bestowed upon his own design work, Alister MacKenzie, writing in 1920, conceded that the "natural features which he so much admired had all been artificially created."

Golf courses have come a long way since the classical seaside links and the modern inland venues. In effect and style, the post-modernist golf course today travels "back to the future."

Cultural Links

When Jimmy Joe LaRossa of Clarksburg, West Virginia hired Pete Dye back in 1978 to turn an abandoned coal field into a golf course, the owner offered to clear the site of rusted mining equipment. Dye told him not to touch a thing. What one person sees as trash, another sees as the raw material of art.

Sixteen years later, the visual effect of such cultural artifacts is now brilliantly—and finally—on display at The Pete Dye Golf Club. A cart path from the sixth green to the seventh tee is actually an old mine shaft that cuts through a mountain of coal. The eighth green sits under an exposed coal seam. Railroad tracks and loading sheds adorn the back nine, and a number of bridges are historic wooden structures that add a creaky feel to the grounds. Even a sixty-year-old haystack and rusted farm implements have been incorporated into the design. Modern energy is also a theme at the long par-five fifth hole, which lines up right into a trio of 800-foot-high smokestacks that rise up two miles behind the green.

Such touches create a distinct sense of place and make a round of golf more enjoyable. There is nothing more disappointing in golf architecture than a layout that appears to have been forcibly imposed upon the site without benefit of attention to native features or culture. This, for instance, is what is so annoying about the Jack Nicklaus-designed Pinehurst National GC in North Carolina. These holes are intended simply to be as tough as possible, with high power fade shots demanded at every turn. When played after a round at nearby Pinehurst #2, where subtle shotmaking and traditional design craftsmanship are the order of the day, the heavy-handedness of a Pinehurst National leaves one with a sense of a morning wasted.

The classic charm of seaside links is that their look, their texture, and their turf are all inseparable from centuries of evolution and history. The juxtaposition of railways and golf courses, such as at Prestwick in Scotland or Royal Lytham and St Annes in England, speaks volumes about how the steam engine linked town and country.

A far more antiquated sensibility is evoked by castle ruins that dot the golf landscape, such as at Lahinch in Ireland or Cruden Bay in Scotland. And nothing can emulate the charm of a golf course like St. Andrews, which derives its power and grace from its location literally in the midst of a medieval university town.

Modern course design, which dates itself primarily from the advent of mechanized earthmoving equipment in the mid-1930s, has always been less sensitive to established features. In large part the problem is simply that so much good land has already been used for other purposes. Yet changes in technique and attitude have also been decisive. The post-World War II emergence of the professional landscape architect was in many ways a logical extension of the triumph of science and machinery over native landforms—and not necessarily for the better.

A survey of course design today reveals that a number of designs excel precisely because they have worked with, rather than against, what was already there. In this sense, the idea of refined course architecture is to enhance an established habitat and to complement local cultural traditions.

No one is more imaginative than Pete Dye in this. At the Indianapolis 500 Motor Speedway, he has rebuilt a golf course that incorporates sections of the old racetrack wall. One par-three is backed up into the grandstand alongside turn number three, and four holes sit on the track infield. Lest there be any mistaking this authentic American landscape, the incoming holes bring into play or view the following structures: high-voltage power lines, railroad tracks, petroleum storage tanks, a barn, and a motel.

A great number of successful attempts come to mind that might serve as models. Dan Maples' The Pit in Pinehurst is routed through the strange dunescape of an old sand pit. Even the tee markers—screws, spikes, and rail anchors—evoke the earlier use of the site. In a very different manner, Jeff Brauer and Larry Nelson designed a golf course for Opryland in Nashville along the banks of the Cumberland River that uses the native limestone bluff as a backdrop for several greens. Little Traverse Bay GC in Harbor Springs, Michigan, uses elevated tees and carefully cut fairway corridors to reveal stunning vistas of the surrounding land. The Serapong Course in Singapore offers a bewildering set of cultural juxtapositions: the front nine is routed through lush, colorful fields of native flora, while the back nine brings the golfer just across the water from a navy yard marked "RESTRICTED ACCESS," and one of the world's busiest container cargo ports.

To be sure, strategy, shot-making, and course conditioning are important to sound design. But beyond that, the imaginative use of native objects and features contributes to successful architecture and makes for more interesting golf. Such are the cultural links that make the game so different from other sports. The joy of a round, after all, is not simply the golf, but the visual imagery and the sense of a distinctive experience of place that four hours outdoors ought to bring.

Routing Is Destiny

The most important element in planning a golf course is the routing of the holes. Other components—the selection of grasses, the length of the course, the position of hazards and artificial mounds—are all secondary to the basic issue of how well, or how poorly, the holes are positioned in relation to the land. That's why designers, or at least their associates, spend countless hours pouring over topographic maps and making different suggested "footprints" of the holes. An architect who doesn't sweat over this process isn't worth the money he or she is paid.

A case of flawed design routing can be found at a classical old Canadian layout, the Vancouver Golf Club, host of the LPGA's 1991 duMaurier Ltd. Classic. The course dates back to before World War I and was built entirely by hand labor, with no earthmoving equipment. The 160-acre site is bisected by a huge rolling hill that runs on a north-south axis. To avoid the problem of sidehill billy-goat fairways, the designers wisely chose to route all but one of the holes east-to-west. From tee to green, the tee shots are generally uphill to the crest of the hill, and many of the approach shots play downhill.

So far, so good. But when you're cutting fairway corridors through dense virgin woodlands that far north, you don't have much sunshine that can reach down into the tees and greens tucked into the woods. With holes that run east-west, the holes are deprived of sunshine because during peak daylight hours, the sun is tucked behind trees. The result is that for years, quality turf at Vancouver GC has been at a premium. It seems that new greens are continually being put in, with the result that the putting surfaces have an inconsistent feel to them. Superintendent Bruce Thrasher is performing miracles to get the course in shape, but his biggest battle is with the routing.

Bloomingdale Golfers Club, just east of Tampa, Florida, sports an engaging design on flat land. But architect Ron Garl committed a no-no when he laid out the par-four opening hole due east into the early morning sun. Another basic rule of course routing, by the way, is not to build the 18th hole into the setting sun.

Most of the time, course routing is determined by what the developer wants. The highest hill on the property might be an attractive place for a clubhouse, but that can often mean that the 9th and 18th holes have to play steeply uphill. Another serious problem is posed by land developers who designate the areas for residential properties and then hand over the rest of the land for an architect to do his work—usually on broken land that drains poorly and offers few interesting features. The only way to avoid such disasters is for a developer to call in an architect at the outset of a project, before the master land planner has chosen the residential lots. It also helps when architects can press their case with their client and make a claim for quality lands.

It's always interesting to see a good piece of golfing property compromised by a weak routing. New South Wales Golf Club, just south of Sydney, Australia, would have a far better reputation worldwide as a seaside course if its holes more closely adhered to the natural dunes and swales of the land rather than crossing over the ridges at 90° angles.

There are all sorts of formulas for routing. The classic links style is to have the ninth hole at the far end of the course. The modern routing runs two nines, each starting and returning at the clubhouse. A fine version of this can be found at Muirfield in Scotland, where the front nine is a large clockwise loop that wraps around the incoming nine, which runs counterclockwise.

Among the basic rules to follow are that holes with similar lengths and playing characters, for instance, short three-pars or reachable five-pars, should run in different directions; it's preferable to avoid driving areas that run up against a perimeter fence on the right; holes that switch back in direction are preferable to those linked in a line like sausages; long four-pars should not be built into the prevailing wind; and the opening holes ought to be kept relatively free of massive obstacles and hazards.

Two Donald Ross-designed courses in Connecticut built during the 1920s display ingenious routing features. At Wampanoag Country Club in West Hartford, all of the short par-fours run uphill. The Country Club of Waterbury, seemingly slight at 6,301-yards, par-69, turns out to play very much longer because nearly all of the tee shots play into soft fairway rises that effectively deaden the ball.

The most important rule of all is to keep the land interesting. Anyone can build a hole like Cypress Point's 16th, where the famed par-three green sits out on a natural rocky peninsula. The real trick in routing a golf course is to make consistent use of terrain that is not well-suited to golf.

Yale Golf Course in New Haven, Connecticut is 17 holes of melodrama, but the 18th is undoubtedly the world's worst finishing hole for such an impressive layout. Perhaps architect Charles Blair Macdonald ran out of dynamite, or money, or maybe he always wanted to create a 616-yard five-par requiring a forced carry on the second shot over a sheer rock ledge 80 feet high. Years ago it could be considered "a sporting hole." Today it's the result of poor planning that left him on unplayable ground.

The basic routing only works when it includes a thorough incorporation of wetlands, construction contours, available sunlight, drainage patterns, shot-making balance, and an internal rhythm to the succession of holes.

A final note. There's nothing worse in golf than a formula or cookie-cutter program. The Old Course at St. Andrews breaks every rule of design balance. There's something to be said for whimsy, or the deliberately odd. That's what distinguishes the great, memorable courses from merely functional ones.

∞

Movers and Shapers

Golf course architects rightly get a lot of attention in terms of basic design work. But when it comes to implementing the plan and converting two-dimensional drawings into three-dimensional golf space, the true captains of dirt are the shapers.

Shapers put into final form the features that give golfers headaches or elicit sighs of appreciation. They operate the rattling heavy equipment that turns raw land into golf holes. They can use the eight-foot blade of a bulldozer to nudge a golf ball down a fairway. Ask anyone in the business and he'll tell you that the shaper makes or breaks the architect. Jay Morrish, a veteran Texas-based designer, calls them "Rembrandts on dozers."

The work involved in building a golf course is overwhelming. It is common today to move a million cubic yards of dirt during construction of a course. Imagine a cube 100 yards per side—the length of a football field. Fill it up with dirt and you've got a million cubic yards. The trick is to spread that pile of dirt around so that it looks like naturally flowing golf ground compatible with the surrounding terrain.

Andy Banfield, formerly a shaper and now a design associate with Tom Fazio, calls it "massaging clay." "You have plans on paper," explains Banfield, "and you're trying to fit them into the third dimension, so everything has to be shaped and refined. The real interesting features come in when you get into vertical space. You just keep massaging those edges until you get them right." The shaper is the extension of the architect's hands and mind. "They're the folks who put that certain look into it that golfers will remember," Banfield says.

Shapers have no unions and no formal accreditation. Many are comfortable as freelancers. Fifty-one-year-old Marvin Schlauch, a former highway hand from Ohio, has for 20 years carried a business card that identifies him as a "professional greens builder." These days one of his steady clients is New York-based architect Stephen Kay.

Schlauch is short and stocky, with a gnarled, weatherbeaten face. He has an idiosyncratic golf swing, characteristic of someone with no formal training in the game. But his innate feel for golf is evident in his work at the Boston Corners Golf Club in Millerton, New York, a private course that Kay designed on the estate of electric equipment manufacturer Stan Peschel. It's a nine-hole course with double sets of tees and double greens so that it plays as if it had 18 holes. A golfer going around the course the second time plays from different tees to different sides of the greens.

Schlauch stands on the 15th tee and proudly points down to the green, 179 yards away, which doubles as the putting surface for the par-five 500-yard fifth hole, coming in at a right angle. "That ridge there," Schlauch says. "I ran that in and it's all you need to keep those two holes from ever playing as one."

The informal rule in the business is to start someone on a wheeled vehicle—a tractor or dump truck, say, then move him up to a front-end loader. Next stop might be one of the machines used for cutting and filling: a track hoe, for instance, which is a backhoe mounted on a track assembly. Then it's time for real earthmoving. The basic piece of equipment is a D-8 bulldozer, a $250,000, 32-ton monster with a blade eight feet wide that can push eight to ten cubic yards of earth at a time. Next are the slightly smaller John Deere 850, 750, and 650. Finally, the shaper moves on to "light" equipment, such as the Caterpillar D-3. The smaller the machinery, the tougher it is to operate. (Don't ever say "drive.")

Good planning supposedly makes accurate cost estimates possible and forms the basis for selecting a contractor through competitive bidding. Still, many decisions inevitably end up being made in the field, and that can drive prices up fast. "The arm-waving period," Robert Trent Jones, Jr. calls it. "Clients hate it," he says. "A wave of the left arm can cost $5,000."

Strangely enough, the worst place from which to view a golf course is the control panel of a bulldozer. The operator straps himself into a seat in a metal cage atop the machine. The engine sits up front and precisely blocks the operator's view of where the blade is cutting. All that a shaper can see are the corners of the blade poking out from behind the motor casement. There are no orientation points, no levels or markings, no mirrors. The only way to get a rear view is to twist around and look back over one's shoulder. Chronic backache is a shaper's occupational hazard.

An awkward level on the left controls the throttle and the forward or backward directions. On the right is the stick for lifting and tilting the blade. Pedals control the steering. The dozer spews out vast amounts of heat and dust and makes enough noise to drown out one's thoughts. A nice, quiet 12-hour day on the golf course. Getting to this enviable position takes years. You start with a shovel or rake in hand and work your way up the ladder. Mike Strantz, now an up-and-coming course architect in his own right, was on the maintenance staff at Inverness Club in Toledo during George and Tom Fazio's renovations prior to the 1979 U.S. Open. The construction crew couldn't quite capture the old Donald Ross feel there, so Strantz took a rake and began smoothing the outline of an unfinished bunker by hand. The foreman, Andy Banfield, liked what he saw, and Strantz joined the Fazios as a shaper the day after the Open.

The bigger construction companies are constantly on the lookout for new talent. The most respected of American course contractors, Wadsworth Golf Construction Company of Plainfield, Illinois, employs 35 full-time shapers, each earning from $45,000 to $80,000 a year. Wadsworth dispatches them in teams of two to four to any of its 20 or so ongoing projects.

Every architect has to establish a working relationship with the shapers. Because jobs are usually won through bidding, architects don't always get the shapers they want. Sometimes they'll present the client with a wish list and hope for the best. Occasionally an architect gets stuck with an inexperienced crew that he has to supervise with painstaking care. This can cause a lot of friction and may dictate many more visits and many more dollars than initially anticipated.

Chances are that if the holes look like runways, they were built by a road-construction crew that brought in the lowest bid but had little experience in golf. That's why many architects prefer to use their own crews when they can. In Japan and throughout Asia, where construction crews often require moving 2 million to 3 million cubic yards of earth, there are skilled native operators of the heavy earthmoving machinery but few with the ability to do the final shaping. American designers take their own shapers on jobs in Asia. They get $4,000 to $10,000 a month plus living expenses and two trips home per year. A job typically lasts four months, but it's common for crews to go directly from one project to the next.

When it comes to taking a hands-on approach, Pete Dye is the master. On Kiawah Island, South Carolina, just below Charleston, Dye set up shop on a four-mile stretch of dunes along the Atlantic. There, for a fee of $250,000, he worked at breakneck speed getting the site ready for the 1991 Ryder Cup matches. Dye is like no other architect. In fact, he's not an architect at all. He's a builder. He literally moves in, then spends every daylight hour knee-deep in the muck. He arranges leases with local suppliers for equipment, and he can operate any piece of machinery on the grounds. He makes no drawings and uses no topographical maps. When negotiating with environmental regulators he likes simply to walk them around the site and explain what he's doing, incorporating their concerns as he proceeds.

Dye's chief shaper at Kiawah Island was Tom Simpson. He was once a farm laborer in his native Montana, running small tractors. While earning a B.S. in horticultural landscape at Montana State, he spent a summer on highway construction. During his senior year he turned up at a local golf course that was under construction. "I watched the shaper and fell in love with that kind of work. I just thought it was the greatest thing in the whole world."

After graduation, Simpson landed his first job—maintenance at a golf course in Colorado. "I wasn't qualified to work with a designer, so I figured I'd get in on the ground up." After a while the superintendent asked Simpson whether he'd had any experience operating bulldozers; Perry Dye, a Denver-based contractor/designer and Pete Dye's son, was recruiting shapers.

"I couldn't really operate a dozer, but I knew my way around the machinery," he says, "so they sent me to San Diego to learn how to shape. Pretty shaky at first, but I got the hang of it. Four months later they shipped me to Japan.

"I worked two years there for Perry on four different projects, and then returned to America for a while. In late December 1989 I was planning to go back to Japan and came to Kiawah to see what Pete was up to. The day I got there just to poke around, this D-8 arrives. Nobody could operate it. Pete asked Perry if he could use me for a week. A year and a half later we were done. I guess it turned into a long week."

Good shapers are hard to find and a lot harder to keep. They have a silent hand in building the world's best (and worst) layouts, and they deserve credit (and blame) for their efforts. No doubt, the designer is in charge; after all, he's the one to sue. But architects could never convert their dreams into reality without the skills of bulldozer operators. The next time your perfect chip shot runs off a green into a hazard and you find yourself cursing the architect, save a few choice words for the shaper.

⌒

Who Cares About Teeing Grounds?

H ere's a good way to mess up your golf game. Next time you prepare to hit your opening drive, spend some time thinking about the golf tee; not the wooden kind, but the ground you're standing on. Is the teeing area square or oddly shaped? Is it inclined or dead level flat? Does it point in the right direction, or 20° off-line? If that doesn't ruin your round, chances are, nothing will.

If you never gave the teeing ground a moment's thought, you wouldn't be alone. Until halfway into the nineteenth century, standard practice was to commence the next hole within a few club-lengths of the previous hole. Sand was dug out of the putting hole and gathered into a little mound, the ball was placed on top of it, and presto, that was a tee. Small wonder that over the subsequent decades, the original term "tee" branched off and acquired two distinct meanings: the wooden peg from which the drive was played, and the area of managed turf from which that shot was struck.

Today, the design, placement, and construction of the teeing ground has reached scientific proportions. British architect Fred W. Hawtree, in his treatise *The Golf Course: Planning, Design, Construction and Maintenance* (1983), devotes 23 pages to the subject. When it comes to golf, everything is by design.

The model for the modern tee was established at St. Andrews in the mid-nineteenth century when greens and fairways at the Old Course were expanded into their present form. Formal teeing grounds were established alongside greens, in some cases on a smooth turf that was merely an extension of the putting surface.

Over the years, the shape of tees has changed dramatically. It was not enough that they consist of mowed ground. As golf designers began to create courses inland, where the natural conditions for golf were nowhere as favorable as on seaside linksland, they had to take into consideration the mundane topic of drainage. Teeing grounds were especially prone to becoming waterlogged. They were basically level and provided no surface flow for runoff. Over time they became worn down into a saucer-like shape so that water puddled up in the middle.

Just after the turn of the century, golf gained in popularity with the advent of the Haskell rubber-cored ball. As play increased, it was no longer sufficient to provide a single strip of teeing ground. The turf would quickly wear out. Greenkeepers adapted to the new demands by building larger tees. This meant that tee markers could be moved both up and down as well as across the newly enlarged teeing grounds.

The classical designers gave no thought whatsoever to the strategic placement of forward tees. H.S. Colt and C.H. Alison make only one passing reference to the subject in their *Some Essays on Golf Course Architecture* (1920). Their design associate, Alister MacKenzie, basically neglected forward tees altogether in his work at Cypress Point. Donald Ross, by contrast, often sketched out forward tees in his design drawings, though his explanation for doing so in his book, *Golf Has Never Failed Me* (1996) has more to do with altering the hole day by day (and different wind conditions) than in adapting the course for variously skilled golfers.

After World War II, golf became very much a power game. A premium was placed on length. Robert Trent Jones typified this approach with his use of excessively long tees that gave a particular hole maximum stretch. But it also tended to give the hole a boring look. When a teeing ground is more than 30 yards long, a player standing at the back of the tee has trouble seeing the landing area. The feeling is less of golf than of standing on an aircraft carrier. Building one tee may simplify a maintenance program, but why seed, water, and mow huge areas that are hardly if ever brought into play? Gradually, tees were broken up, into either the free-flowing forms devised by E.L. Packard in the 1950s or into smaller teeing grounds relied upon by Pete and Alice Dye beginning in the mid-1960s.

Today, the trend is toward multiple tees, often four or five per hole. This gives a course flexibility for championship play, low handicappers, seniors, and women. In breaking up tees, designers are also introducing varied angles of play. From one tee, there's a forced carry of 200 yards, while from another, placed 50 yards forward and 20 yards to the right, there are options that offer challenges without requiring heroic shots.

Stand on a tee and think about the variables that go into its placement and shape. Does it line you up reasonably square to the target, or is it pointing toward a fairway bunker, or worse yet, out of bounds? Is it wide enough so that instead of playing over trees on the right you have options to tee the ball up to the left? Perhaps the tee sits astride a property line, and a steep hill abuts the line of play. Sometimes, a tee is nestled so deeply in a grove of trees that it is cut off from sunlight and has turf starving for sunshine.

Over the years, course design has made a number of advances. Among the most important, and the least recognized, concerns the shape of teeing grounds. As with so many aspects of architecture, the golfer doesn't take notice until he or she comes upon a botch-up. When done right, the teeing ground draws attention not to itself but to the landing area, the hole, and the natural surroundings.

Save Us from Green Committees

For the integrity and well-being of the golf course, it's often best to keep the green committee as far away as possible. Yes, of course there are those members of the board who have managed to do the right thing. But in my visits to private and public courses I have seen some of the wildest things done by some half-cocked green chairman armed with a bright idea.

I have several standouts in my "Hall of Shame" when it comes to bonehead redesign. At one blue-blood club in the Northeast, the esteemed members managed to destroy an eccentric old par-five that used to call for a drive over two bunkers in the middle of a saddle crossing the fairway. The members apparently tired of walking over or around the hill and simply put a paved cart path right down the middle of the landing area, between the two traps.

At another club, originally designed by Donald Ross, a former club bigwig and nationally-ranked amateur took out dozens of bunkers, all of them on the left side of play. Needless to say, he played a draw shot and tired of having to make so many recoveries from bunkers on that side of the green. On another hole, the club was "looking for more yardage" and so added a new back tee to the club's shortest par-four; the effect was to turn a distinctive drive and pitch hole into another indistinguishable two-shotter.

The list goes on: deciding to add a lake, replete with fountain and railroad tie walls, on an inland course otherwise without water. And of course there's the catchall solution, of adding another tee to create distance. In the absence of available acreage, one can always toughen up the green by building goofy mounds from outer space. And then there's the classic strategy of "beautification": add trees. When in doubt, plant more of them. Who cares that in 30 years, wide-open areas will end up playing like paths through dense jungle?

Members often call for changes, too, so let's not leave them out of the picture. The course is too hard, so let's cut down the rough. The greens are too slow, so let's make them faster. What matter if the course was constructed with putting surfaces pitched at 4 or 5 degree slopes. The main thing in the modern game is to have fast greens that register 11 on the Stimpmeter.

And green fairways. The model for this comes from the high-rise office building, with its totally controlled atmosphere of closed windows and climate control through simultaneous air-conditioning and heating. Likewise with the golf course. Keep it green with saturation watering, then complain about the *Poa annua* buildup, so put more drainage in and then water it more to keep it lush and plush. And then run thousands of golf carts indiscriminately over the softest areas, or better yet, build more cart paths.

Three cheers also for those who would "modernize" their

golf course. Oh, those antique mounds on the third fairway! Why, they just get in the way; let's level them.

Okay, you get the point. If a green committee isn't resisting all these changes, it is not doing its job.

That doesn't mean never change the golf course. It simply means to manage the change carefully. A golf course, after all, is an organic object and changes every day on its own. With refinements in the game and in maintenance practices, it would be foolish to pretend that we could stick our heads in the sand or just place the golf course on a museum pedestal.

The trick is to plan for the long run. It's called developing a master plan. Instead of the green committee voting to add a big bunker on the 14th hole, it should hire an architect or a consultant and devise a five- or ten-year vision. This prevents the crazy in-house politics of green committees that have torn many clubs apart with screwball plans and last minute dues assessments. Instead, let it all fall into place with a vision, a long-term budget, and a set of priorities.

In securing the services of an architect, clubs should take the trouble to inspect other work on similar courses that he or she has done. Don't just take their word for it, go out and look at it personally.

Most importantly of all, educate the members. Green committees, course superintendents, club pros all must play an active role in helping the membership cultivate a sense of the treasure and worth of their home ground. Spread the word on the club's design history. Post the original blueprints in the bar. Prominently display old photographs of the golf course. Have the golf pro take members on a walk to show them features of the course—odd mounds, weird angles—that perhaps are little understood in terms of strategy. And most of all, encourage among the members a keen sense of the value of playing a great golf course for its own sake and because it makes the game more fun.

The most interesting golf courses in the world—St. Andrews, Pine Valley, Pebble Beach—attained their reputations because they are more interesting to play the second time around than the first. The shots are memorable, and no matter how well—or poorly—you play, you appreciate the variety and dexterity they call for. That's what an appreciation for course design is all about. Why shouldn't your course be the same way?

∞

Trees on Golf Courses: Do They Really Belong?

It's easy to get upset about trees on golf courses. After all, from a classical point of view, they simply don't belong. A golfer will survey the likes of St. Andrews, Muirfield, Dornoch, and Prestwick and find there not a single tree in play. What, then, to do with the well-known American proclivity for fairways lined with conifers and hardwoods? Or, to take one very bad example, a towering pine tree smack in the way of the approach shot to the green at the 465-yard par-four (!) 16th hole at Spyglass Hill in Monterey, California? Gentlemen, start your chain saws.

All of us know about golf courses routed so narrowly through corridors of trees that they must be played single file. Architects lacking in imagination (and construction budgets) might try to pass this off as "challenging." The real challenge of such layouts is how their designers manage to keep finding work.

There is some sort of strange emotional attachment that club golfers have to their favorite oak or maple, even when it stands smack in their way and they stumble into it every time they play a hole. Just try cutting it down and the members will rise up and revolt.

Yet when ample playing room is provided, a course framed with graceful trees affords some of nature's loveliest ground. A high backdrop of trees creates a stage-like setting for fairways and greens. The effect is all the more apparent when the foliage changes in mid-stream, such as at Cypress Point. The transition there from towering pines to gnarled, wind-blown cypress trees marks a dramatic shift in the surrounding landscape, from parkland to oceanside.

There's no reason a golf course can't be an arboretum. Superintendents learned a generation ago to avoid relying upon one dominant species. When Dutch elm disease ravaged the country, it destroyed the character of many courses in the Midwest and Northeast. The value of diverse stock is evident today at Cranwell Golf Club in Lenox, Massachusetts. Its parkland atmosphere and mixture of hardwoods are due in large measure to the late nineteenth century landscape work there of Frederick Law Olmsted. Ash, hickory, maple, oak, and even a precious American elm behind the eighth tee create an admirable variety of color and texture without in any way cluttering up the golf shots.

Elm trees, by the way, are the perfect golf tree because they provide shade and yet their natural umbrella-like canopy allows easily for play underneath. Few courses today are lucky enough to have any of them remaining, one glorious exception being the Country Club of Detroit, where 80 elms—out of 600 originally there—survive to grace the grounds.

When the likes of a Winged Foot or Oak Hill were built in the 1920s, their sites were basically barren. Extensive tree plantings were in order. Today the great skill is not in aggressively planting but in prudently trimming limbs and removing trees. The golf course, after all, is in a constant state of organic evolution. Trees get larger, the canopy of leaves begins to close in on fairways, and problems of air circulation and limited sunlight can exact their toll on turf.

Great damage can be done to the integrity of a golf course in the name of ornamental tree planting. Sometimes, the argument is for "safety" between holes. Other times, the membership is determined to make—or keep—its golf course "tough." But too often, the plantings detract from the design. Among the worst offenders are those firms specializing in course "beautification." One of the most prominent of these, run by well-intentioned folks who neither golf nor understand golf strategy, consistently recommends an aggressive program that becomes tantamount to filling up every available space, even if it means dopey little Christmas trees 10 yards off a fairway.

One telltale mistake that results is the tree placed so close to a fairway bunker that it results in a "double-hazard" whereby golfers are faced not only with a long sand shot but with having to negotiate (i.e., carry) a tree placed directly in front of them between the bunker and the green. Another basic fault is the tree canopy that so closes down upon a tee that the leaves on both sides join down the middle, and the effect for the golfer is having to drive underneath the double overhang, as if playing through a tunnel.

Often, the encroachment is less the result of invasive planting programs than the gradual outcome of isolated decisions. Consider Wannamoisett Country Club, a Donald Ross-designed gem just southeast of Providence, Rhode Island. The greens there are among the purest putting surfaces in golf, and Ross surpassed himself in deploying a variety of green contours, including a punch bowl, inverted saucers, and subtle fall-away slopes. Yet there is all too much evidence of recent tree plantings, many of them alongside the landing areas of tee shots, or to block long hitters from carrying the inside of doglegs. Such tampering gradually puts at risk a wondrous piece of natural strategic contouring and subtly forces its artful ground game into a less subtle version of modern target golf.

The proper use of trees starts with the routing. No topographic map or aerial photo can tell the architect what he'll find on the ground. That's why it is crucial for designers to walk the site repeatedly before a single hole is routed. There is no more exciting stage of design than bushwhacking through thickets of woods and stumbling upon a truly memorable specimen tree worth preserving—or better yet, routing a hole around. The key is leaving room for options, and not simply forcing players, or at least the heroic ones, into airmailing shots over leaves and limbs.

Besides, trees that impinge too much on a golf course merely exaggerate the difference between low-handicappers and higher-handicappers. Strong players can usually get the ball airborne and thus play over trees, whereas weaker players struggle to get the ball in the air at all. Why further punish the high-handicapper?

Several fine examples of good tree strategy are on display at the Pete Dye-designed Blackwolf Run-River Course in Kohler, Wisconsin. It's a stunning layout, bold in its lines and dramatic in the use of elevations. It especially works because holes 5 through 13 along the Sheboygan River appear as if Dye had meticulously peeled away the existing foliage and placed the holes in the midst of it. At the center of the triple fairway at the 337-yard par-four 9th hole is a stand of 90-foot high cottonwoods. Thus the name of the hole, Cathedral Spires. These trees create all manner of options off the tee—safe left, a power fade, or a bold draw over the stream.

Trees alone on a golf course are not a virtue, and can in many cases simply obstruct play. The real issue is integrating them into aesthetics and strategy. As in all enduring works of landscape, the golf course demands vivid imagination to reveal nature's grace.

Golf Courses and Old Ballparks

It is World Series time. Thoughts naturally turn—momentarily, of course—from the golf links to the baseball diamond. It does not take long to realize that when it comes to the nature of their playing fields, the two sports have much in common.

The overall dimensions of the fields differ for every venue. Each outfield is distinctly shaped, just as each golf hole has its own look and playing characteristics. With baseball, as with golf, no two sites are alike. Each field is unique, and he or she who masters it and gains that uncanny home field advantage will enjoy a certain competitive edge over visitors. Most importantly, the affinity of golf and baseball derives from the fact that in both cases, the point is to advance a ball across vast open spaces by virtue of a club swung by the upper body. The ball rockets skyward, and the beauty of its distant flight is perhaps the most inspiring of each game.

But the similarities go beyond these formalities. They have to do with the style and specific characteristics of each field of play.

The great thing about golf is the sight and feel of the course. In an early morning dew, the grasses and leaves fairly twinkle with the light of the rising sun. Late in the afternoon, with the shadows long and bold, a rolling layout takes on the appearance of some strange new creature.

With shifts in the weather, the golf course assumes any number of personas. Nothing is more invigorating than to play a single round of golf under several markedly different conditions. This is the particular magic of seaside courses, because their proximity to the wilds of wind and water assure variety on an hourly basis.

Inland courses offer an entirely different aesthetic. Here one finds not fluctuation but solidity: a grandeur and stateliness of trees and rolling terrain. Everything speaks of permanence, a quality one sees in such unshakable monuments as Augusta National, The Country Club (Brookline, Massachusetts), or Southern Hills in Tulsa.

The best golf courses embody a distinctive feel and sensibility. There is no mistaking where you are when you play Cypress Point. The same goes for the work of the classical architects. The greens at a pure Tillinghast course look and feel like no other. Witness, for instance, Brooklawn Country Club outside Bridgeport, Connecticut. The routing of the holes is not particularly inspired, but that's not Tillie's fault. He was presented with the layout in 1929 and asked to redo the greens without touching the routing. The result? Greenside bunkering and putting surfaces that leap out at a player for their boldness and originality.

What does this have to do with baseball? Simply that the classical ballparks were unique. Just to enumerate the old baseball palaces is to conjure up reveries of endless hours spent before the radio or, if lucky, in the grandstand. Sportsman's Park in St. Louis. Shibe Park in Philadelphia. Pittsburgh's Forbes Field. Or that house of bedlam in the naked city, Ebbets Field on Flatbush Avenue in Brooklyn, where a player who hit a ball at the haberdashery advertisement in right field could win a free suit from Abe Stark of Pitkin Avenue, "Brooklyn's leading clothier."

Cincinnati's Crosley Field is gone. The place sat only 29,000 people, and its center field wall was but 387 feet from home plate. But it had that steeply inclined left field terrace—in lieu of a cinder warning track.

The quirkiness of a 37-foot high left field wall at Fenway Park is a part of baseball's charm. So, too, is that right field upper deck in Tiger Stadium, Detroit, where the stand overhangs the field. Sometimes, it's the whole stadium that's eccentric. Witness the old Polo Grounds, the world's largest shoe box.

The oddities of baseball architecture create a kind of excitement sadly lacking in modern parks. Perhaps, then, it was a fitting touch of baseball nostalgia when the refurbished Yankee Stadium opened up again in 1976; the fencing atop the length of the bleacher wall was the same gilded facade taken down from the old roof.

Today, one searches desperately for such touches. Pittsburgh's Three Rivers Stadium is simply indistinguishable from Veteran's Stadium in Philadelphia or Riverfront in Cincinnati. Instead of the famed little "jury box" bleacher in Boston's old Braves Field there's the unrelieved symmetry of an Atlanta Fulton County Stadium. There used to be a strange concatenation of outfield fencing. The new fields offer nothing but perfectly contoured dimensions devoid of any character. Half the time, now, the turf is artificial, and the trend is toward indoor, domed fields as well. Seattle's Kingdome has all the ambiance of an industrial warehouse. Welcome to the great Northwest?

Baseball has suffered for these modern, soul-less buildings. They're no longer made just for baseball; they're multipurpose and thus lacking in ambiance. Instead of sitting literally on top of the field looking straight down, you are now a long way away and forced to follow the action on the video scoreboard.

Golf has suffered a similar fate. The overwhelming majority of golf courses being built in the celebrated boom era of architecture have been lifeless, undistinguished tracts. Instead of the PGA Tour playing its Kemper Open at Congressional, it has gone down the street to the TPC at Avenel, a paradigm of golfing emptiness.

Tournament courses supposedly designed for spectators offer nothing by way of memorable shot-making, except for anxiety-provoking photo opportunities. The subtlety is taken out, the quirkiness and the texture are gone. Technically brilliant these new courses may be, but filled with character they are not.

All is not hopeless. Pilot Field, the new baseball stadium in Buffalo, New York, built for the Pirates Triple-A team, the Buffalo Bisons, started the revolt. Here is a new facility built to look like an old one, replete with arches and facades and seating that cozies up to the field. The park holds all of 19,000, but for several years running now, season's attendance has approached if not topped one million—a minor league record.

In its wake came Baltimore's Camden Yards, a return to the virtues of industrial and urban eccentricity with intimate seating and a classical sensibility. The "retro-look" has also inspired new ballparks in Cleveland and Arlington, Texas, much to the delight of both ball players and spectators.

Let golf course architects take a lesson here. Old-looking can also be beautiful. The classical style does strike a responsive chord with the public. And it can be more fun to play. Give me daytime ball at Wrigley Field. And let me have one of those classical old venues at 6,300 yards where they didn't move any earth around and where they didn't have to build in ungainly water hazards. I want a baseball diamond with real grass, and a golf course with greens the character of Ebbets Field.

The Incredible Shrinking Clubhouse

There's no need for the clubhouse to be an oversized wedding barn. Far too many clubs have mistakenly thought they'd gain credibility or status with some outlandish steel and beam structure designed to make the cover of *Architectural Digest*. Along the way, they can't even pay their house bills. Besides, nobody joins a golf club for the clubhouse, and if they do, they've joined for the wrong reason.

Example: Ironhorse GC, West Palm Beach, Florida, the case study for John Strawn's book, *Driving the Green*. The text explores course architect Arthur Hills' attention to environmental sensitivity, yet nothing in the manuscript prepares visitors for the sight of an overstuffed, blue-roofed modernist clubhouse that looks like a garden shed on steroids.

I know of one fine layout where the management has so bungled matters over the years that the club, already deeply in debt, borrowed over one million dollars for a clubhouse expansion. Today, the club pays more in debt service for the interest on its note than it spends on maintenance for the golf course.

The aristocrats who took early to golf created some legendary clubhouses. Shinnecock Hills, National Golf Links, Baltusrol, Winged Foot, Chicago Golf, Medinah, and Riviera all sport buildings of historic design merit. When golf took off after World War I, social activity centered upon clubhouse life because private clubs served as a refuge from Prohibition. The post-World War II era saw a more sober approach to clubhouse construction, but the speculative boom of the 1980s unleashed a whole new wave of flashy money that developers eagerly sank into opulent palaces such as Troon G&CC in Scottsdale or Castle Pines outside Denver. It now appears that golf's "edifice complex," like corporate America generally, is going through a downsizing. Clubhouses are becoming leaner and simpler as the game returns to basics.

Consider the recent portfolio of Atlanta-based Diedrich Architects, one of the country's most respected clubhouse design firms. Up through 1991-92, it completed massive buildings at TPC-Summerlin in Las Vegas (35,000 sq.ft.), English Turn in New Orleans (42,000 sq.ft.), New Albany CC outside Columbus, Ohio (50,000 sq.ft.), GC of Georgia (52,000 sq.ft.), and Admiral's Cove in Jupiter, Florida (60,000 sq.ft.).

Thereafter, its standard clubhouse shrank dramatically: Champion Hills in Hendersonville, North Carolina (25,000 sq.ft.), Collier's Reserve in Naples, Florida (21,000 sq.ft.), Augustine GC in Washington, D.C. (12,000 sq.ft.) and Deer Creek on Skidaway Island, Georgia (11,300 sq.ft.).

Why the incredible shrinking clubhouse? As usual, economics. The golf course market is changing, with a decided shift from real estate-driven private clubs to a greater share of self-standing, daily-fee facilities in which the main attraction is golf. For another, there's less money to be made in food and beverage operations. The historically lucrative liquor trade has fallen some 30 percent at private clubs in the last five years owing to greater awareness, and enforcement, of DWI laws. Moreover, changes in federal tax law have slashed deductions for the kind of business entertainment that had long been the mainstay of private clubs.

The bigger the clubhouse, the higher the overhead and the higher the dues must be. No wonder so many members are finding that their total costs per round exceed $200. The high-end market can bear only so much weight. Moreover, reducing clubhouse size has a significant effect on start-up costs. Even though smaller clubhouses cost more per square foot to build, the overall savings are considerable: a 50,000 sq.ft. clubhouse costs about $115 per sq. ft. to build (total: $5.75 million), while a more modest structure, say 15,000 sq.ft., costs $135 per sq.ft. (total: $2.025 million). On top of that, there's less to spend on furnishing, utilities, and labor once the building is in operation.

Increasingly, clubs are reporting that instead of building huge fixed structures, they're relying upon tents and outdoor patios for the occasional large function. It makes little sense to hold bar mitzvahs simply to meet overhead. Nor any need to build marble staircases and hand-polished sushi bar locker rooms when the money could be spent on the golf course—or not spent at all.

There's something classy in a subtler approach to the game. That's why the tastefully designed Atlantic Golf Club (1992) out on Long Island, New York, offers a traditional East End shingle design clubhouse with no ballroom or evening dining.

Just in case you ever lose touch with the game, you can head up to The Orchards, a 1922 Donald Ross-design gem in the college town of South Hadley, Massachusetts. The wooden, two-story clubhouse, no more than 6,500 sq.ft., offers old-fashioned cozy charm of the sort that you'd find at your basic Scottish links: lockers with metal grill fronts, a ramshackle restaurant upstairs, and a patio overlooking the course where you can relax and have a can of beer. Back to basics, indeed.

∽

The Tyranny of Yardage

In the mid-1970s, when Johnny Miller was winning PGA tournaments with scores of 24- and 25-under par, his caddie, Andy Martinez, would give him distances to the half yard. Forget about eyeballing the shot. The pros today demand precision.

The reliance upon yardage is part of a powerful trend in golf. The game has become aerial, with players needing to know how far the shot is so they can fly the ball all the way to the target. We are now beyond the point where cart paths are sign-posted with distances. The whole golf course has been measured, lasered, and subject to satellite surveillance, with each cart equipped with a computer monitor that informs golfers of the precise distance between any two points on the hole. The USGA has lost control of such devices and given way completely. They should have stepped in years ago and put a halt to all means of measurement.

The problem is that more and more, golfers are playing automatically without getting the feel of the shot. The art of inventing shots and of curving the ball in or bouncing the ball up to the hole has been lost on today's players.

Jack Fleck, 1955 U.S. Open champion, takes credit for first having used regular distance charts while playing the tour in the 1950s. Jack Nicklaus, who needed all the help he could get to compensate for notoriously poor eyesight, popularized them in the 1960s. But until the mid-1970s, caddies were responsible for mapping out their own distances. Depending upon the caddie, the quality of yardage varied markedly, from a single cryptic notation on a scorecard per hole to the elaborate, multi-colored foldout pocket albums perfected by Ernest "Creamy" Caroline, Arnold Palmer's longtime bag-toter.

Nothing was worse for a caddie than to be caught in the fairway with "bad yardage." Gradually, the yardage notations became standardized. The breakthrough came in the mid-1970s when "Gorgeous" George Lucas found he could make more money selling yardage maps at each PGA Tour stop than he could carrying a bag. For a while in the early 1980s, the PGA Tour took over production of these maps and supplied them at each event. Yardage maps are now mass-marketed. Perhaps the best in the lot is the Strokesaver series, which features durable glossy booklets of the world's most prestigious courses.

Yardage makes for automatic golf. There's no need to size up the shot, no need to worry about the lay of the land. It also fits in nicely with a series of related developments which have helped promote a mechanical swing style. The advent of the metal-shafted club effectively rendered obsolete the classical handsy, sweepy swing. The golf swing became upright, with "dead hands" the rule and the emphasis upon hitting the ball high.

Changes in maintenance techniques encouraged this style of play. Rough-to-rough watering created a lush, plush turf on which the ball would not roll. Greens were also kept soft and receptive for high shots. The result was a move away from the ground game and the emergence of more target-oriented golf.

Golf design responds to changes in equipment and swing techniques. Modern golf has become an airborne power game in which the ball is flown all the way to the designated landing area. That's why architects end up building narrow ledge greens, with forced carries over water and sand the rule. The widespread use of three wedges has simply confirmed these trends. It's one thing to guess at a short lob shot, quite another to pace off 73 yards and then fire away with a crisp 60° lob wedge.

A quick look at the older courses shows, by contrast, that their entrances have been left open so that players can "ramp" the ball up to the putting surface. Golfers today who "risk" low-running bump-and-run shots from 90 yards in are looked upon by their playing partners as miracle workers—or as antiquated fools.

No wonder, because today's ever-present island or peninsula green would not have been playable in an era of estimated yardages. Players now must know that the forced carry is precisely 172 yards.

Here's a way to recapture a sense of golf design and basic principles of land. Next time you play a round, forget the yardage map, turn off the onboard computer, and eyeball each shot. By (re)creating the ground game, you'll develop a keener sense of your home course, or of any course. You'll also be forced to manufacture shot-making. Instead of needing a map to play, you'll only need your head.

Some day soon, when courses have to rely upon less water and when the turf will be kept dry and firm, golfers will have a chance to experience the virtues of the ground game. A good way to start is simply to turn one's back on the tyranny of yardage.

∞

Don't Make Me Ride

Relying upon a cart for a round of golf is like watching other people have sex. You get a distorted view of the course, and it alienates you from the experience of actually playing the game.

The late Bill Diddel, an Indianapolis-based course architect, used to call golf carts "wheelchairs." When I started caddying at private clubs in the late-1960s, members could only use golf carts with written certification by a physician. Even then, they had to take a caddie along. Now, it seems, even the most physically fit men and women regularly toss their golf bags on a cart and head down the fairway.

The price of living in a free country, I suppose, is that if people want to ride, they should be allowed to. As a distinct minority, golfers have rights, too.

But consumer choice does not exist in a vacuum. We are, after all, the most automobile-dependent countries in the world. It's no surprise that we have mechanized our outdoor leisure. When club managers, course owners, and club pros discovered in the 1960s the bottom-line advantages in golf carts over caddies, the fate of walking was sealed forever. Unless, of course, players fight back.

A special curse is reserved for courses where riding is mandatory. There is no excuse for this greed, and golfers should simply demand the right to walk. If their civil rights are not upheld, then perhaps a boycott is in order.

I can already hear the litany of responses. "It would slow up play." "The walks between greens and tees are too long." "We can't recruit caddies," and "Pull carts don't look dignified." As if an armada of golf carts did!

First, there is no evidence that golf carts speed up play, especially with the need of late to keep golf carts confined to curbed cart paths that run along one side of the hole. Has anybody scientifically studied how much real walking players do when they keep their carts on the designated paths? I have seen all too many players who didn't know how to position their carts properly, didn't take the proper clubs with them, and then returned to their carts for their putter after chipping to the green. This slows up play.

Second, the widely recognized decline of golfing etiquette today is partially attributable to the negative cumulative influence of golf carts. Why do so many golfers today not rake bunkers, not replace divots, and yet manage to tromp all over putting lines when on the green? It's because they never got the training and practice that caddies did, and so when they learned the game—usually not until their mid-20s—they weren't fluent in the game's subtle manners.

Third, the last thing I want to see when looking at a golf course is a cart path. On the very first hole at Eastern Michigan University's Huron Golf Course, a daily-fee facility in Ypsilanti, a cart path intrudes between the fairway and the fairway bunker. Sadly, it's an appropriate start to a course whose prime function is to move golfers through rather than make them feel as if they're playing a proper layout.

Cart paths in the line of fire are only good at scramble events, when the last player in the group can try for a 400-yard drive by playing for the blacktop. Far better are such courses as The Links at Spanish Bay, or Port Armor in Georgia, where the cart paths, hidden behind soft mounds, turn outward and away from the tees and then return inconspicuously to the landing areas; out of sight and mind.

Fourth, golf carts destroy the rhythms of the game. They unsettle the game's pastoral grace, and make it difficult to think about the last shot or to plan the next stroke.

Fifth, nobody calculates into the equation how much it costs to build and maintain paths and to repair all the damage from carts. Sure, carts generate revenue, but development costs. An extra 10 acres, paving, mounding, costs close to half a million dollars at the outset that has to be paid off over the years. Plus, the areas around cart paths and those sections of the golf course generally subject to traffic have to be maintained and repaired, and yet no one calculates these costs into the mix.

Finally, reliance upon carts makes it impossible to appreciate the natural beauty of the course. Holes are designed to be seen from a height of five or six feet, not from a sitting position. It is simply impossible to assess angles of play, the nuances of the land, and the contours of the fairway or green when riding along in a golf cart.

There's no turning back the clock. Golf carts and cart paths are here to stay. But don't make carts mandatory. Keep paths out of the way. And give people the freedom of choice.

The ideal would be to make caddies available. A number of resorts and private clubs throughout the country have developed and maintained extraordinary caddie programs. Pebble Beach, The Inverness Club in Toledo, and Pine Valley in New Jersey come to mind.

If it's too much work to create a caddie program, then just set a single price for green fees, cart included, and let golfers decide whether to walk. Requiring players to take a cart as a means of generating additional necessary revenue is just a way of passing off upon the public a system of irresponsible and misleading financing.

There is no finer experience in the game than playing a round accompanied by a qualified caddie. It's also an indispensable means by which the game can recruit a new generation of players. But in the absence of caddies, I'd happily settle for the right to take a pull cart or carry the bag on my shoulder.

Thank Heaven for Little Four-Pars

We're seeing a turn away from length. Strategy—and therefore options—are once again in vogue. The evidence is especially clear when we look at what's happening with par-fours.

Pete Dye may have hit the matter on the head when he said that we have witnessed the death of the long four-par. Nobody on the PGA Tour has to hit a long-iron anymore, except for the second shot on a par-five, and now it appears that Tiger Woods is also putting the lie to that.

Perhaps the most amazing thing about Robert Gamez's tournament-winning eagle deuce on the 18th at Bay Hill in 1990 is that it is no longer a big deal when a golf professional hits driver and seven-iron to a 456-yard hole. High-handicappers are sweating out their second and third shots to the greens while the modern professional has managed to tame holes of enormous length.

For about two generations, architects tried simply stretching out the tees. The effects were devastating in several ways. A lot of fine 6,300-yard courses built on 100 acres of land became considered obsolete. Some of the new elongated tees looked more like airport runways than the starting point of an interesting golf hole.

Long holes are boring, or at least they are interesting for only some of the players some of the time. There is very little joy in watching a world-class player hitting a full second shot to a par-five and coming up 90 yards short of the green. The best thing that ever happened to tournament golf was the advent of the reachable five-5, what came to be called the par 4 and 1/2. One of the many ways in which Augusta National revolutionized course design was by championing the cause of the short five-par. The beauty of Gene Sarazen's double eagle in 1935 on the 15th hole was that in going for the green he courted disaster. And that, after all, is what strategic choices are all about. For every one under pressure who makes it over, there's a Curtis Strange (1985) or Seve Ballesteros (1986) who dumps it in the water or a Chip Beck (1993) who plays it safe.

Besides, reachable five-pars are fun for middle-handicappers who can have a fair go at the green in two, achieving, for the moment, anyway, what they have dreamed about for years.

The same now goes for the short four-par. If length does not intimidate the pros, why not finesse them to death? Throwing in a Lilliputian par-four here and there also breathes new life into that great majority of us golfers for whom a green hit in regulation and maybe even a birdie are the exception rather than the rule.

Famed old Prestwick GC in Scotland demonstrates that what we now call short four-pars were very much a part of the game in the days of the gutta-percha ball. A drive of 180 yards was an achievement in the days of Old—and Young—Tom Morris. Small wonder that written accounts of golf at the Old Course at St. Andrews do not have to offer special explanation when detailing how a player got his third shot over the burn fronting the green at the 370-yard first hole.

Today, St. Andrews has three of the best drivable four-pars in golf. Depending on the vagaries of the wind, of course, the strong player can usually have a go at one of the holes by the turn: the 9th at 307 yards, the 318-yard 10th, or the devilish 12th hole, only 316 yards.

The 9th is perhaps the most maddening par-four in the world. The fairway bunkers end about 60 yards short of the green, and the putting surface and approach area are dead level flat; nothing more than a huge patch of mowed-down fairway. With the wind behind you and the ground characteristically firm, there's a strong temptation to fire away on the drive. Heavy gorse bushes loom down the left, and should you come up several dozen yards short you have the most impossible shot in the whole game. No elevation change, no apparent break. You could putt, chip, bounce it in, or hit a full wedge. I have seen single-digit handicappers flub, shank, whiff, foozle, or simply blade this second shot, and more often than I can count they wind up with a five or a six when minutes earlier on the tee they were thinking of a two.

At the Old Course at Ballybunion, the 361-yard sixth is not reachable off the tee, but it does display many strategic virtues. There is a modest leftward drift to the fairway and out-of-bounds tight on the right. The unbunkered plateau green cants right to left. Behind, there is absolutely nothing. Three or six, what is it going to be?

Alister MacKenzie, with perhaps more wisdom than any other architect, had the nerve to build back-to-back short four-pars at Cypress Point, the eighth and ninth. Together, these two holes through massive dunes are some of the most compelling 625 yards in golf.

This is no mere ode to the past. Witness the 14th hole at Tom Fazio's Lake Nona course, opened in 1986. The downhill 287-yard 14th is right out of Pine Valley, though Fazio rejects the idea that he had any one course or ideal in mind when he built this fabulous little hole. A huge fairway bunker lines the right side; behind it, impenetrable woods. The green sits in a hollow, fronted and flanked by steep bunkers with water wrapping around the landing area from the far right and running behind the green.

The safe play is an iron to the left. But what fun can this be when compared to the risk of a hard sliding drive that trickles onto the green? A pure case of the strategic principle: in going for two, you risk running up a seven. It is a hole that anyone can play and have fun on. And that, after all, is what sound strategic design is all about.

Don't Call Them Women's Tees

Golf course architect Alice O'Neal Dye likes to tell of the time she met the women's committee at an esteemed Northeast golf course that had brought her in as a consultant. Some of the committeewomen were elderly golfers who had known the course for decades. "They told me," Dye says, "that they loved their course just as it was, that it already was the toughest in the area, and that they didn't want a thing changed."

"I appreciate that," Dye responded, "but you ought to know that your golf course has been changing for years. Take your first hole. It's 340 yards from the forward tees. Back in 1940 you were driving the ball 160 yards on average. The ground was firm, virtually unwatered, and the ball would roll on and on. You had a good chance to hit the green in two. In 1950 they installed an irrigation system and you lost 15 yards on the drive. In 1960 they converted the fairways from bluegrass to lusher bent grass and you lost another 15 yards. In 1970 they decided to toughen up the approach shots by adding that bunker in front of the green and now you have to fly your *third* shot to the putting surface. And all the while the trees that were mere saplings grew and spread so that the effective landing area was narrowed down from 60 yards to 30. You say you don't want the course changed? Where were you when the course was being changed?"

Alice Dye cares about women in golf like no other course architect. She was the first female member of the American Society of Golf Course Architects. She has published widely on the need to design courses for the modern woman's game. And yes, she does have the ear of her husband, Pete Dye. Pete listens because Alice Dye is analytical and knows exactly what she's talking about.

Alice Dye doesn't see the problem as merely women vs. men. According to her, all players, men and women, should be accommodated. The basic problem is that golf today is increasingly becoming a game of strength. Those who are less strong, whether women, seniors, high-handicappers, or juniors, all suffer on the golf course.

First of all, not all women are equal in golfing skill. Why should there be two or three separate tees for men and only one for all "ladies," regardless of whether their handicap is 4 or 36? Yes, it's good that there's a forward tee for women. But there really need to be two tees for them as well.

And please don't call them "Ladies' Tees" or "Women's Tees." Dye, along with the USGA, suggests we call them "forward" or "red" or anything but "women's."

Today, the differences between all players, including men and women, are greater than ever. Dye points out three developments that have decisively reshaped the game. The first involves course maintenance. Courses are slower than they were 50 years ago. The ground game has become an aerial game. Courses are lusher, irrigated, often overwatered, and seeded with grasses that are thicker—and therefore slower—than before. The ball doesn't roll as far as it used to. Instead it has to be flown and then it hits and stops, in dart-like fashion. This works to the disadvantage of players who are less physically strong.

Second, golf equipment today favors power, too. All of the recent advances in golf balls, shafts, and clubheads favor those who hit the ball hard and who can strike the ball cleanly and firmly. Women and older male golfers, claims Dye, gain nothing in distance from these developments. Low-handicappers benefit some 5 percent, while the top level amateurs and pros gain closer to 10 percent. So the gap between stronger and weaker players is growing.

Third, the demography of golf has changed. Fifty years ago few seniors played. Today, 30 percent of all rounds are played by those 70 years and older. In years back, the average female golfer was a "sportswoman," an all-around-athlete (remember Katherine Hepburn in the 1952 movie, "Pat and Mike?"). Today, with increased leisure time and the liberating effects of the women's movement, more and more nonathlete females are taking up the game, especially at private clubs. And the cart has enabled them to play without having to exert themselves at anything like the levels necessary when they would walk or even carry their own bag. On average, claims Dye, the golfers are more varied by both age and physical skill than years ago.

While these developments implicate all golfers, they affect women more than men. What's needed, argues Dye, is a greater attention among designers and green committees to the diverse needs of different genders, different ages, and different physical skills.

The ideal solution is to provide multiple tees, four or five being ideal. The trouble along the fairway should come into play for the longer hitter, not the weaker, because longer hitters are stronger players and they can extricate themselves from steep bunkers and heavy lies, whereas weaker players cannot. And at greenside, there ought always to be an alleyway open so that you can get the ball onto the green by rolling or bumping it, not simply by having to fly it.

Some may disagree, claiming that in golf, as in life, the

strongest should prevail. Alice Dye dissents. Trends in contemporary architecture confirm her: multiple tees, less forbidding trouble for the high-handicapper, and courses that do not automatically reward length or punish the shorter hitter.

5

Business or Art?

Working Landscapes

The modern golf course is a curious combination of engineering and artistry. When it comes to drainage, for instance, the water has to run downhill. As for growing turf, it's a matter of fitting the right grasses to the proper soil and climate. But that's only half the achievement. The real creativity comes when it's time to build something that's beautiful and memorable—and that functions as well. That's why it is helpful to think about the golf course as a working landscape.

It isn't enough to say, as many have, that "form follows function." All too easily, this can become—as it did in the 1960s and 1970s—a formula for merely functional golf courses, designed to expedite play-along rather than to inspire golfers. If the form is entirely to be determined by function, then the most logical outcome is to plow ahead with holes that do not impede play, with greens large enough to capture all but the worst iron shots, with bunkers removed from the right side of play, and with cart paths flush alongside the fairway in order to get players through as quickly as possible. Come to think of it, that's what a dozen or so third-rate architects have been doing for years.

Thankfully, some course designers today are moving away from such nonsense. Flowing features, greater attention to contour mowing and sculpted bunkers, and freer form to tees and greens: these are some of the welcome trends that have helped enliven the design craft in the past decade or so.

In golf, as in any creative endeavor, of course, it remains notoriously difficult to talk about what counts as "art" or "the beautiful." But perhaps the effort is worth trying. To start with, a golf course is a landform that integrates with its surroundings. This natural setting—the sense of place, both visual and cultural—sets the tone for the golf course. The vast open spaces of a mountain setting establish a context for dramatic holes that call for bold carries deep into the third dimension. By contrast, seaside holes are routed to accommodate the dunes and native winds.

The setting frames the holes and gives us a sense of place. A stone wall may help define a New England golf course, just as a distant barn may orient a shot in the dairy lands of Wisconsin or Minnesota.

The artistry here is to embed a course within a distinct place. As Desmond Muirhead reminds us about St. Andrews, the medieval university town serves as backdrop for the Presbyterian morality play of the Old Course. The names of key features tell the religious tale. From the soft repose of Elysian Fields, it is but a short step into the damnation of Hell bunker at the 14th. And the very end of the journey forces us to confront the terrifying Valley of Sin.

Architects today have little control over the setting, but they have virtually unlimited control over landforms. While some designers like to emphasize natural sites for greens and tees, others champion the modernist cause of using technology to do the work. Pete Dye has always been proud to claim that his layouts are artificial. And Bob Cupp is perhaps the game's leading advocate of computer-aided design and aggressive earthmoving in the search for aesthetic landforms.

Cupp's art school training as an illustrator and oil painter attuned him to the artistry of course design. While working as club pro in Florida in the mid-1960s he found his ability to draw an advantage in planning some course revisions. It wasn't long before he landed some design work, and then spent nearly two decades as one of Jack Nicklaus' most trusted associates.

Cupp's work shows an enormous attention to creative landforms. He has championed the use of mounding to create shadow effects on the golf course—witness such Nicklaus designs as The Bear in Michigan, Loxahatchee in Florida, and Desert Highlands in Arizona.

On his own since the mid-1980s, Cupp's recent work reflects this attention to making the golf course visually stimulating while keeping it playable as well. Port Armor, 75 miles east of Atlanta on Lake Oconee, is perhaps the most varied example of this attention to bold styling. His Marietta Country Club might exude the same look if it were properly maintained.

There is nothing in recent golf design that can prepare one for the steamy swamp look of Settindown Creek Golf Club in Woodstock, Georgia (since 1995, home to the Nike Tour Championship). Except for the downhill roller coaster 18th, the holes are basically flat. Yet Cupp has built counter-slopes, forced carries, ramps toward the green, and so much lateral motion that the holes remain endlessly fascinating to walk and play.

Moreover, Settindown benefits from varied playing textures, and this is the final element of artistry in course design. There is nothing more numbing than a golf course that is uniformly lush. Members might like the look, but no one would want to visit, and those who do end up checking their watches around the seventh hole in anticipation of getting the round over. The endless fascination with links courses lies in their varied plant materials and surfaces. Multiple colors, different feels, dynamic looks in different seasons: these are what help make a golf course beautiful.

Today, more than ever, golf courses are underappreciated as natural assets. Birds and other wildlife thrive on them, they cleanse the air, absorb sound, and moderate heat.

As environmental assets, golf courses are recreational sites as well as artistry in their own right. In an economy seeking to develop tourism, what better way to create jobs, preserve open space, and build something that is lovely to look at?

☙

Golf Design Goes Ivy League

Anyone who enjoys being an armchair architecture critic should spend two days at Harvard University's Graduate School of Design with Professors Cornish and Graves. The professional development seminar, offered annually since 1985, draws aspiring golf course designers to sweat over topographic maps, slide shows, and hour after hour of fascinating lectures.

Masters of ceremonies in 1991 were two of this country's most experienced golf course architects, Geoffrey Cornish of Amherst, Massachusetts, and Robert Muir Graves of Walnut Creek, California. Together, these two have been responsible for over 800 golf course designs and renovations. Not that they have set any trends, nor for that matter, built anything more than functional golf grounds. Though their respective designs lack the most elemental verve, and they each have exceeded their share of clumsy holes, they do have something to say about course planning and construction technique. They are also both past presidents of their profession's leading institution, the American Society of Golf Course Architects (ASGCA).

Instead of lecturing in academic cap and gown, they donned their society's traditional red wool jackets adorned with the traditional Ross plaid, in honor of ASGCA founding member Donald Ross. They spent a total of 16 hours laying out the basics of their craft, and left the audience wishing that the seminar could have gone on for a week.

"Golf Course Architecture 101," it was, with just enough detail on such arcane topics as master planning, bunker construction, and subsurface drainage to make participants think they were qualified to go off and do their own courses. But of course, they (we) were not. The beauty of the whole experience, besides the friendships made, was the excitement of realizing (once again) how immensely complex the whole task is. The real miracle is that so many good designs are planned, built, and maintained.

At times it was like Bob and Ray, or perhaps Bartles and Jaynes. Cornish and Graves know their material inside out. While they follow the extensive lecture notes handed out in advance to seminar participants, there's a humorous give and take between them, with Cornish making repeated reference to wayward shots that Graves has allegedly hit on various historic courses. Meanwhile, Graves points out to Cornish that malpractice insurance doesn't normally cover the case of someone getting hit by an off-line shot on an architect's course. Cornish then promised to reread the fine print on his contract.

The audience included a diverse lot from the golf world. There was PGA tour player Lon Hinkle, fresh from having overseen a design project in Montana and now looking to come in from the cold. Mark McCormack's influential agency, International Management Group, sent a representative, doubtless to front for IMG's impressive stable of stars looking to get into the design business. Paul Azinger Golf Course Designs sent two. Golf project managers from Israel and Thailand were there to learn more about the design craft. And among the half dozen women in attendance was pro golfer Cathy Cook.

Cornish, co-author (with Ron Whitten) of that indispensable research work, *The Architects of Golf*, gave a helpful overview of the history of golf course architecture. Graves then sent everybody into a panic by assigning them the task of routing 18 holes over 300 or so acres of rough terrain. It was truly "back to school" for grown men and women reduced to penciling in tees, fairways, bunkers, and greens and coloring them in with an assortment of Magic Markers.

Sounds like fun, and it is. But then there are just a few guidelines to follow. This was no back-of-the-napkin doodling at the 19th hole.

The acreage and topography, based on an actual California site, turned out to be not so generous. Eight areas were specially designated Native American burial sites and could only be excavated on the basis of costly (and time-consuming) interventions by local councils. Slopes of more than 10° grade had to be avoided altogether.

Then there were concerns about the amenities: access roads were more or less fixed; specimen trees needed to be respected (and, ideally, preserved); the practice area ("Don't ever call it a driving range," admonished Cornish) should be placed in a northerly direction in order to maximize use; and east-west holes were to be avoided wherever possible.

We were also advised to make the first hole a moderate "getaway" hole not facing into the rising sun. Then there was the "Cornish rule": to make sure the first five holes ran in at least three, and preferably four, different directions. Also, we were not to run the par-threes and par-fives in the same direction. Tees were to be placed about 50 to 100 yards from the last green. We needed to keep the playing area some 420 feet wide at the landing area. And then a few questions, like where to site the clubhouse and maintenance buildings. Could the practice tee, 1st and 10th tees, and 9th and 18th greens all be seen from the starter's box? All this while keeping open the possibility of someday developing homesites.

In addition to this exercise, both Cornish and Graves presented detailed talks on the whole process of construction— clearing, grass selection, greens mix. What came through is how much this is a "hands-on" business. Architects must, of course, be salesmen, but they aren't worth much unless they also are "dirt men." No matter how much classroom time is accumulated, this is a trade learned in the field.

Graduates of the program now know the answer to a question recently raised by a prominent monthly golf magazine: Whatever happened to the classic old blind hole, such as the hidden green at the par-three 6th at Lahinch in Ireland? Modern earthmoving equipment today gives designers possibilities that were unimaginable a half century ago. Besides, the liability insurance premium alone on such a hole would likely bankrupt a club today.

Golf design involves business, aesthetics, maintenance considerations, and the politics of green committees. Cornish and Graves gave workshop participants a fascinating look at how these elements interact.

∽

When Business Threatens Art

An awful lot of modern golf course design is taken up with the business side of things. There's big money, after all, in some of today's projects, and a lot of people are investing heavily in hopes of a profitable outcome. In part, it's a matter of moving pricey real estate lots. It's a lot easier justifying tens of millions of dollars in start-up costs (and $300,000 for one-acre plots) when the project bears a big-name designer or the golf course is promised a national ranking.

There are also enormous competitive pressures today that have fundamentally transformed the design profession. It is now standard operating procedure for designers to have publicists, photographers, and promoters on board as part of their office entourage. What with overhead costs today of setting up shop—computers, blueprint machines, liability insurance, medical coverage, and office rent—it is no surprise that architects are anxious to keep a steady flow of work going just to pay the bills. A number of designers report that the technical side of actually doing a job proves easier and less consuming than the politics, schmoozing, wining, dining, and dealing involved in landing those assignments in the first place.

There are also more designers in business today than ever, though the amount of work nationally has remained about the same for the last decade. Those who head their own design operations accept as a matter of fact that the associate or design assistant they bring on board today might well become tomorrow's competitor.

Looming over the whole industry is the concern that independent course architects, good skilled visionaries though they may be, will find it harder to get jobs when they go up against big-name golfers who try to cash in on their name recognition by going into the business as so-called "designers." It's one thing to have won a U.S. Open or Masters, and quite another to have mastered the enormous details of landscape engineering, agronomics, drainage, and environmental science that are basic to golf design today. Yes, a few have mastered that path, but the vast majority of such "names" are really fronting for a behind-the-scenes crew that is doing the day-to-day work. Designing a golf course cannot be done from cellular phone calls between tournament stops.

More than anything else, designing a golf course is a matter of aesthetic sensibility. That's what makes looking at classical designers such a refreshing and educational experience. Sure, Donald Ross, A.W. Tillinghast, and Alister MacKenzie were competitors, and they were keen to be paid for their services. But they were also artists, and instead of relying upon cheap trademarks and signatures they allowed the integrity of their routing and its subsequent shaping to do the speaking for them.

Their works defy a simple formula. Those who claim today, for instance, that there is a classical "Ross" bunker or green are really trying to position themselves as experts rather than explaining anything meaningful about the original. Ross flashed sand up when he needed to create definition, and he also created flat bunker floors when he thought the sand might not hold up against the bunker wall. As for the analogous claim, that Ross always crowned his greens at the back, a careful look at the wondrously diverse putting surfaces at Wannamoisett CC near Providence, Rhode Island, will disabuse anyone of such simplicities.

For all the ability of modern equipment to move heaven and earth in construction, nothing beats the brilliant use of a rolling plot of ground. Tillinghast, at Five Farms north of Baltimore, for instance, created holes that move effortlessly and naturally without the slightest trace of a forced march. The best—or is it the worst?— example of how contrived modern design can be lies literally next door, at the club's West Course, where Bob Cupp and Tom Kite collaborated on a golf course that for all the evident earthmoving and shaping is simply at odds with its natural setting.

The shame of it is that so little remains of the original masterworks. A fascinating manuscript by Geoff Shackelford on the limited design career of George C. Thomas, Jr. demonstrates that of the 10 or so courses he did between 1904 and 1928, only Riviera CC in Los Angeles comes close to embodying its original. Many of Thomas' inventive holes, with double fairways and bold angles of approach to greens, have been eviscerated by various committees and lesser talents who destroyed what was most distinctive in such once-brilliant Thomas layouts as Los Angeles CC-North Course, Bel-Air CC, La Cumbre CC and Ojai Valley Inn G&CC in California. Nor does there seem much evidence that recent "restoration" efforts at Bel-Air and Los Angeles by the likes of Tom Fazio and John Harbottle even approximate the original design genius.

It is sad to have lost such works. Part of the genre's traditional fount of wisdom and inspiration is thereby removed forever. The art of architecture becomes impoverished each time a modern designer tears into the work of a classical golf course— in far too many cases, without the new architect even bothering to research thoroughly the original. These were pioneer designers, after all, who worked with their imagination rather than with massive equipment. Their task was to make the most of the land rather than to reinvent it. In an era today when so many courses look like they were airlifted in, and when the price of their construction too often includes bulldozing all that was most distinctive about the site in the first place, it is always refreshing to see the quirky genius with which classical designers practiced their art.

Nor does it have to be one of the big names. There is far more to be learned from the design works of a Seth Raynor, or even from the late-1920s architecture of Wayne Stiles and John Van Kleek, than from the vast majority of "signature designs" so heavily marketed today.

CR

Oh No, It's the PGA Show!

A defining moment for me during the 1995 PGA Merchandise Show, held—like all of them now—at the mammoth Orlando Convention Center, came when a young entrepreneur buttonholed me in an attempt to get some free publicity. Unable to afford the requisite fee for a booth, or perhaps like so many others merely shut out from those precious few 2,762 available spots, he obviously had practiced at getting his sales pitch down to a ten-second sound bite.

"With this new computerized display board in your golf cart, you can preview the golf hole before playing it. It also works as a two-way communications system with the pro shop, so you can receive messages, get weather warnings, or order lunch."

Wow! And to think I've been playing golf for a quarter of a century without it. No wonder my game suffers.

Actually, after two days of walking the floor of this seven-acre floating bazaar, all I really suffer are sore feet. And a longing for golf as a simpler game. But who's kidding whom here? No matter how many times Old Tom Morris rolls over in his grave, the golf market isn't going to go away. Too many people are making, or trying to make, too much money for things ever to get simple again.

Figure it this way. The game generates about $25 billion in revenues per year in the U.S. Averaged out, that means 500,000 people are each grossing about $50,000 annually from the game. Okay, Greg Norman and Mark McCormack make much more, while those guys raking bunkers down at Palooka Hills Muni make a whole let less. You get the point. Just check out those fancy cocktail parties (fresh shrimp, not frozen; and open bars, no chits) at The Show. Someone want to tell the sales reps for Club Car, Izod, or Aldila that they can't be in on the game?

Indeed, the only people who don't benefit from golf during

The Show are those who try to collect green fees at Orlando area courses all week. We're talking about serious freebies. That's half the reason why folks get into this business in the first place. Rounds are comped. Free sleeves of balls, shirts, and hats, too. You get to travel, and down the road there's always hope of hobnobbing at The Masters.

So what if you can't break 90? That's how golf differs from every other sport. You don't have to be a professional athlete to be inside the game and a part of it. Of all those folks over at the Super Bowl party, how many actually play football? Even touch football? Same in baseball or hockey. Their stands are filled with wanna-bes, could-have-beens and, most of all, never-weres. They just passively "spectate" and watch others play the game.

The beauty about golf is that those who surround the game and cash in on it also play—maybe not well enough for the PGA Tour, but surely well enough to enjoy themselves outdoors. So stop worrying about all the hype and high-tech breakthroughs, revolutionary designs, and fluff about "longest golf balls." If someone wants to flail away with a punk rock Death Stick driver, let him. And if someone else needs to measure his yardages with laser accuracy, well, now he has a chance.

All these ridiculous gadgets and inflated promises of a better game are harmless enough. They're best thought of as entertaining ways for folks to find their way into the golf business. That way, they, too, can travel around and get comped at golf courses. It sure beats working for a living. No wonder so many people are willing to sleep out overnight at The Show just trying to line up a booth. It's just too bad that along the way, the game gets more cluttered, expensive, and commercialized.

⌒

For a Good Time, Call
1-900-CONSULT

A s a golf writer I get some weird phone calls. The other day
a complete stranger rings me up to report about an old
nine-hole course he's found, with another 100 acres across the
street. "I figure I can add another nine holes," he confidently
announces, "and there's still plenty of room for 80 or 90
houses." Would I be interested in investing, or could I help him
raise $2 to 3 million? He's excited because it's a waterfront site,
which I then suggest might be a problem because of environmental regulation. "Na," he says, "they won't give me any trouble." Oh, okay.

It's always amazing to me how many people have this
dream of building their golf course. And who can blame them?
It's all part of the game's charm. The difference, of course, is
that golf development is a very serious business, with all sorts
of technical demands, financial risks, and uncertainties
through permitting. No wonder so many middlemen are getting into the business.

A consultant is someone you hire when you can't figure out
who you should hire to do the real work. How else to track
down the army of people you need today: the golf course architect, clubhouse designer, land planner, surveyor, hydrologist,
traffic engineer, road contractor, lawyer, soil expert, herpetolo-
gist, financier, irrigationist, and resident archaeologist?

Oh, how I envy the classical architects. The likes of C.B.
Macdonald, Alister MacKenzie, A.W. Tillinghast, and Donald
Ross enjoyed great freedom between the World Wars. If they
didn't like the piece of land they were shown, they simply suggested another site down the road.

Permitting? Consultants? Regulatory process? The amazing
thing about golf course architects today is that they can come
up with so many fine courses at all amid intense scrutiny.

Course architects are like artists, except that someone keeps moving the canvas, another tinkers with the palette, and yet another is controlling which paints can and can't be used. To be sure, too many new courses do not measure up, in large part because corners were cut or there was perhaps not enough genius on hand to work through the site constraints. But that's not an argument for junking most of governmental regulation. Golf courses today are undoubtedly more environmentally friendly than they were 40 or 50 years ago. The point, really, is that the creative vision of design newcomers such as Dwight Neville and Douglas Grant at Pebble Beach or George Crump at Pine Valley also requires professionally trained experts and business people. In short, the rules of the game have changed—forever.

One way to deal with this is to hire a golf course architect who really cares about the game and who continually studies golf's subtleties and traditions. Sure it's a business, and technical expertise is needed. But golf demands something more. It requires more than postgraduate degrees, glossy brochures, impressive looking "feasibility studies," promises of "Scottish-style" pot bunkers, or the claim that having won major golf tournaments suffices to qualify you as a designer.

No army of consultants can provide what sound design has always required: a considerable measure of genius, built upon immense technical knowledge, coupled with an enduring love of the game, and the commitment to stay on-site to use that talent.

∽

Lethal Links?

It's enough to give sudden death a whole new meaning. When Canadian golfer Richard McCullough broke his driver over his golf cart in anger over a poor tee shot, the fractured shaft whipped back and fatally punctured his neck. In the summer of 1993, tragedy struck at a private club in Westchester, New York, when a member accidentally heeled his drive and sent the golf ball behind him to an adjoining green, where it struck and killed another member.

A pesticide called chlorothalonil, frequently used on golf courses, allegedly induced such a violent allergic reaction on the part of Navy Lieutenant George Prior a decade ago that he died within a month of his round at Virginia's Army-Navy Country Club. And two years ago a Florida jury absolved the Palm Beach National Golf Club in West Palm Beach for the death of a golfer who had been bitten on the course by fire ants.

This is the game that's supposed to be relaxing? Dr. Keizo Kogure, a Japanese sports physician and author of "How to Die Early by Playing Golf," reports that every year, some 4,750 golfers die on his country's courses. Not, mind you that they die *from* golf, though the stress from overcrowded courses and tortuously long rounds appears to be a contributing factor.

At one U.S. public course, a golfer apparently impatient with slow play pulled a revolver on the group ahead and "asked" if he could play through. Wisely, the foursome accommodated him. There was less opportunity to negotiate with the corpse once found on the green at a Florida muni. For two hours, golfers had to skip the hole until officials removed the body. What an inconvenience.

No environment is entirely risk-free, least of all a recreational facility exposed to the elements. Lightning alone claims five or six lives a year on America's courses. Any athletic activity spread over 150 acres of open terrain, with dozens of people dispatching rock hard projectiles at velocities approaching 125 m.p.h., brings with it the possibility of injury. But compared with many other sports, golf must surely count among the safer ways to spend four hours. Indeed, golfers are exposed to greater danger while traveling to and from the course than they are once on the links.

Unless, of course, they go for a ride on the wild side. A municipal golf course in the Midwest sports a section of cart path 80 yards long—at a downward slope of 23 percent. Worse yet, the path leads into a 30° turn onto a bridge. A decade ago a passenger was killed at the site when the driver lost control of his golf cart there.

Golf course safety starts with sound design. At the planning stage, when the basic routing of the holes takes shape, architects try to build safe margins separating adjacent holes. There's no magic number concerning setbacks, but every qualified designer understands the need to provide plenty of room for landing areas. The proliferation of real estate related facilities raises particular issues of buffer zones. It's not only annoying to see a fairway lined by condos; it's also unsafe for homeowners.

Since nearly 90 percent of all golfers fade the ball, a good industry rule of thumb is to avoid perimeter roads on the right side of a hole. It's also wise to avoid shots played across public roads. Despite the charm of blind golf holes on older, more tightly squeezed courses, the fairway or green obscured from a player's line of sight has become virtually extinct. Likewise today for the cross-over shot. It somehow works at the Old Course at St. Andrews or Lahinch in Ireland, but has been done away with on more recent designs.

Some designers won't go near cart paths, preferring instead to leave design and construction standards to engineering firms selected by the course developer. But most architectural firms will have a say in where the cart paths ought to go and how they should be integrated into the overall landscaping and flow of play.

Actually, they are not golf *carts*—they are more properly called golf *cars*. You might not know that from the way some golfers fly around in them, but in fact course owners are becoming more diligent in their monitoring of just how these vehicles are to be handled—requiring, in many cases, that drivers be at least 18 years old or have a valid driver's license, and that there be no alcohol on board.

From a legal standpoint, clubs requiring golf cars and restricting them to cart paths expose themselves to added liability. Cart paths, after all, bring players closer to adjoining holes and therefore closer to oncoming golf balls. A clever lawyer might well argue that an injured golfer had little room to maneuver away from the offending line of fire.

The latest concern when it comes to accident liability has to do with soft spikes. There are all sorts of grumbling about the alleged frequency of people falling down while playing golf in such nonmetallic spikes, especially in wet weather. Yet for all the concern about the new footwear, the biggest source of lawsuits against golf clubs these days is actually claims from those who have slipped in clubhouse bathrooms while wearing traditional metal spikes. One way to limit susceptibility to legal action, by the way, is for clubs not to mandate soft-spikes but simply to prohibit metal spikes.

No aspect of the game is more subject to speculation, rumor, and political dispute than health-related questions of golf and the environment. A 1991 report by the New York State Environmental Protection Bureau carried the lurid title "Toxic Fairways," yet could only speculate about the potential danger of pesticides to groundwater. Meanwhile, research scientists investigating four golf courses on Cape Cod found no currently registered pesticides detected in groundwater at toxicologically significant levels.

To be sure, the golf industry is becoming more sensitive to environmentally healthy maintenance practices. Golf course architect Michael Hurdzan recalls working on a grounds crew in the late 1950s at Beacon Light Golf Club in Columbus, Ohio. "We were using a handheld baking scoop to measure lead arsenate fungicides and cadmium-based pesticides," recalls Hurdzan. "There was no protective gear, and we would mix that stuff in a barrel and inhale it. Man, I'm sure glad those days are over—and that I'm not."

Indeed, maintenance staff crews applying pesticides are now specially trained, in many cases licensed by the state, and outfitted in full protective gear. Most importantly, they're applying pesticides in smaller dosages, and to smaller areas of the country's 15,000 golf courses.

As for ensuring safety, golfers can protect themselves just by using common sense. The overwhelming majority of accidents are due more to inattentiveness than to structural failure. It's still not a good idea, for instance, to lick the golf ball when cleaning it. Or to leave one's cigar on the ground between swings.

∞

Golf and the Environment: Wildlife Refuge or Toxic Fairways?

During the second round of the U.S. Open at Baltusrol in 1993, play was momentarily halted while a deer ambled across the 18th fairway. To some, the sight of such wildlife amid the hubbub of a major golf tournament might have seemed anomalous. But to those familiar with the environmental issues surrounding golf courses, the scene held a powerful image.

Is golf a prime destroyer of native habitat, or a much-needed greenbelt haven and wildlife refuge in overdeveloped areas? Put another way: Was the deer interloping in U.S. Open territory, or vice versa?

The answer might well decide the game's future, or at least, the future of any new golf course facility, as well as the fate of many existing layouts. Those on one side claim that golf courses are the scourge of nature, spoiling pristine habitat that would best have been left in virgin form and pouring out an incessant stream of lethal chemicals that poison our water table and kill off fish and birds.

The Japan-based Global Anti-Golf Movement (GAG'M), for instance, calls for "an immediate moratorium on all golf course development." According to its own 1993 statement, GAG'M rejects "the myth of pesticide-free, environmentally friendly or 'sensitive' golf courses." It says that "Existing golf courses should be converted to public parks," and "Laws should be passed to prohibit the advertising and promotion of golf courses and golf tourism."

Yet anyone who has flown into Los Angeles might look out the window of the airplane at the smog and concrete asphalt and wish that far *more* golf courses had been built, courses that today might stand as preserves of open space. Especially in built-up metropolitan areas, the vibrant turf of tees, greens, fairways, and rough can be a significant source of oxygen and clean air. Courses also serve as greenbelt buffers that muffle sound, retain moisture, moderate temperatures, and provide habitat for fox, deer, fish, and small game. We witnessed a dramatic example of this greenbelt value when fires ravaged Berkeley, California, in October 1991. As wind-whipped flames engulfed nearly everything in their way, golf courses, with their irrigation systems turned on, provided a desperately needed firebreak that at one point enabled fire fighters to hold the line and battle back.

There have been many serious problems. In April 1984, for instance, 180 Brant Canada Geese turned up dead on the fairways of the Seawane Club in Hewlett Harbor, Long Island. The cause of death was a pesticide, diazinon, that had been properly applied to target "hyperoides," an insect that devastates *Poa annua*. Unfortunately, an anticipated rainstorm did not turn up and there wasn't enough time left in the day to put sufficient water on to saturate the ground. The only infraction investigators could find was that Seawane's superintendent had inadvertently allowed his pest control license to expire. The club volunteered a $5,000 donation to a local environmental group. Meanwhile, the product has been taken off the approved list of chemicals applied to golf courses.

But diazinon still is commonly used on home lawns throughout the United States today. Professional landscape maintenance operations on home lawns are licensed, but your average homeowner proceeds virtually unregulated. Indeed, a good case can be made that golf courses are being unfairly targeted for public criticism when there are far greater sources of danger. The country's 15,000 golf courses comprise a total area of about 2,400 square miles, an area about half the size of Connecticut. But there are 36,000 square miles of home lawns in this country—equal to all of Connecticut, Rhode Island, Massachusetts, New Hampshire, and Vermont. There are also some 441,000 square miles of cultivated farmland where pesticide use, though regulated, is still commonplace. Yet no one makes a public issue of it.

Historically, golf courses have been developed as part of the natural environment. No one thought it a problem when seaside tracts such as Ballybunion in Ireland or Cypress Point in California were built. The original land plan for Pebble Beach called for wall-to-wall home lots all along the cliffs overlooking Carmel Bay. Luckily, the Del Monte Company changed its mind, with the result now being that Pebble Beach Golf Links preserves as a public amenity some of the country's most stunning seaside terrain. Today, however, coastal commissions have clamped down on such projects. Even in a golf mecca like Monterey, plans to build another golf course, this one inland through wooded terrain, ran into determined environmental opposition by Friends of the Forest, a group of home owners and local activists, who successfully objected to the planned destruction of 57,000 trees.

The most "natural" golf courses in the world all require a certain amount of chemical treatment in order to preserve turfgrass. On a Scottish linksland course of fescue grasses, a typical fertilizer treatment consists of liquefied seaweed supplemented with sulfate of ammonia, the pulverized hoof and horn of cattle, dried cattle blood, and some potash iron sulfate. All that's missing is tongue of newt. The point is, such treatment has been part of the game for decades.

It was the advent of pesticides after World War II that gave rise to concerns about "golf pollution." A distinctly American obsession with "greener is better"—the best British links courses usually are a dull, brownish green—led to extensive use of chemicals in an attempt to beautify fairways. The goal was to emulate the lush fairways of Augusta National that had captured the golf world's imagination when color television became popular in the 1960s.

In the last two decades, however, superintendents, working with agronomists, have made enormous strides in limiting the application of chemicals. Today, carefully restricted lists limit those chemicals that can be used on golf courses. These chemicals have to be stored in an EPA-approved storage facility that stands alone from both the maintenance building and the clubhouse. Only state-licensed applicators can even handle the chemicals, and superintendents follow a rigorous regimen governing every aspect of the chemical, its use, and the appropriate weather conditions.

Nor is application a matter of routine schedule or blanket treatment. Today, the intended target pest, weed, insect, or disease must exceed a threshold population before chemicals are introduced to a particular spot. Well before chemicals are even deployed, alternative methods are tried. Cultural prevention might include proper watering, fertilization, aerification, traffic control, and using the best adapted grasses for the region. Organic biological controls are also increasingly popular, including bacteria, parasitic wasps, and beneficial nematodes.

Golf courses are also proving to be efficient in processing their own chemicals. A recent independent study carried out by the federal EPA and the Cape Cod Planning and Economic Development Commission concerning four golf courses on Cape Cod, Massachusetts, showed that, under normal maintenance regimens, the leaching of currently used pesticides and fertilizers yields samples consistent with drinking-water standards. Because the sandy soil on Cape Cod leaches through faster than the clay soil found in most of the U.S., the study represents a worst-case scenario and supports industry claims that golf courses are not toxic.

In addition, the United States Golf Association and the Audubon Society of New York State have been collaborating on a program that enhances sound environmental practices, called the "Audubon Cooperative Sanctuary Program for Golf Courses." The program requires a rigorous, long-term commitment involving six different areas: environmental planning, wildlife and habitat management, integrated pest management, water conservation, water quality, and public education.

For years, the golf industry has been on the defensive in demonstrating that golf courses can be environmentally friendly, even though perceptions are nine-tenths of the battle in any political issue. Local zoning boards are happy to issue permits for condos, regardless of aesthetics or impact on the environment, but when a golf course is proposed, extensive protests and long permit delays are the rule. In addition, although two-thirds of the nation's golf courses are in the public domain, and nearly three-quarters of all rounds are registered at public courses, the widespread misconception that golf is an elitist sport has enduring consequences in the regulatory arena.

Leading golf bodies, such as the USGA, the Golf Course Superintendents Association of America, the American Society of Golf Course Architects, the National Golf Foundation, and the Metropolitan Golf Association have undertaken major efforts to change things, principally by conducting more research and publicizing the game as environmentally friendly. The USGA Green Section, for instance, has spent $3.2 million on environmental studies to determine what happens to pesticides and nutrients when they are applied to turf. Results show that when pesticides and fertilizers are properly selected and applied, their environmental impact is minimal. Further research undertaken by both industry and university groups is concentrating on development of nonchemical turfgrass control products, as well as special drought-resistant grasses that would require less water.

One way to appreciate these issues is to see the efforts developers and architects take in planning a new golf course. At the Atlantic Golf Club in Bridgehampton, New York, out on Long Island, for example, two endangered species were found on the proposed site: the northern harrier hawk and the eastern tiger salamander. The design team led by architect Rees Jones worked closely with the Group for the South Fork and The Nature Conservancy in devising appropriate protective measures. Chief among them were 100–200 foot setbacks around wetlands and the reintroduction of native Long Island grasses that had been lost during the many decades when the site had been farmed. Course superintendent Bob Ranum also worked from the outset with ecologists to fashion a turf management program requiring less chemical treatment than had been deployed there for crops.

The presumption among opponents of golf courses is that the existing land was pristine prior to golf course development. Yet as Atlantic shows, careful course planning can actually help *restore* an area's fauna and flora to what existed prior to modernized farming. Here and in other cases, a crucial question when assessing environmental impact is "Compared to what?"

The scientific case has not yet been made that golf courses can provide more ecological benefits than native vegetation or prime woodland. But as developers explore new projects, and as more farmers face bankruptcy and consider turning over their land to alternative usages, golf surely represents an ecologically sound alternative to "going condo" or building a parking lot, shopping mall, or industrial park.

⚬

Appearance and Reality in the Ratings Game

G olfers love courses. No playing fields in all of sports present such a variety of natural terrains for enjoyment. The result is endless difference, and with it, the kind of compelling fascination that makes the game so extraordinary.

Given the beauty of golf courses and the diversity of their settings throughout the world, it is no wonder that so much attention is placed upon various ratings lists. "Top-100" lists abound, as well as "Best in State." It all makes for endless discussion at the 19th hole, most of it in good fun.

For now, let's start with two of the most influential rating systems, the *Golf Digest* list of top-100 in the country and the *Golf* magazine lists of top-100 in the U.S. How are the lists determined? *Digest* relies upon regular reports filed by an army of 535 volunteer raters nationwide, few of them inside the golf industry professionally, and calculates the lists every other year. Six criteria are evaluated on a 1–10 scale as follows: aesthetics, conditioning, design balance, memorability, resistance to scoring, and shot values (which are given double value). The votes are totaled, and then an in-house panel of editors adds their own vote of "tradition" on a 1–10 scale.

Golf draws upon about 75 industry insiders and asks them to select on their own basis from a nominee list of 400+ courses internationally. Courses are graded in report card fashion: A (top-10 in world); B (top-50 in world); C (top 50–100 in world); D (top 200 in world/top 100 in U.S.); E (top 300 world/top 200 U.S.); F (not worthy of top-consideration). Every other year, the magazine comes up with its lists of 100 best in the world and 100 best in the U.S.

Can ratings be bought?

Yes and no. *Digest* has strict guidelines that prohibit raters from accepting anything more than green fees—often, it turns out, for a foursome. *Golf* simply figures that with raters like Greg Norman and Pete Dye, no one could afford to pay them anyway. There is some concern about golf course owners allegedly flying in some raters in hopes of eliciting favorable ballots; which, again, is prohibited. Of greater concern, especially regarding *Digest*, is having regional loyalists, or aficionados of one or two particular architects, who confine their site visits and vote accordingly.

Another sort of "bought vote" is possible in terms of spending millions of dollars in design and construction creating elaborate earthworks, artificially-built waterfalls, wall-to-wall sodding, and the planting of mature trees in order to create the illusion of lushness and "greatness."

Is early hype a problem?

Absolutely. Courses often start off high on the list, then fall to their "natural level." Harbour Town opened in the top 10 for *Digest* and came down to 57th. Haig Point opened at 28th in 1989 and has steadily fallen to 71st. Much the same could be said for Wild Dunes-Links Course in South Carolina and Blackwolf Run-River Course in Wisconsin, and Pete Dye's Ocean Course at Kiawah Island, South Carolina. Even Shadow Creek in Las Vegas, which turned industry heads when it made its debut at 8th in 1993, fell back the next time around to 17th. Caution is advisable here, though, since we're talking about 15,000 courses. Even the 100th sits comfortably among the top two-thirds of one percent (.0067) of all courses in the country.

Are the lists "manipulated?"

"Early hype" is why *Digest* has now imposed a mandatory five-year wait before a new golf course is eligible for the list. It's a way of preventing its own raters from getting carried away with the latest from Jack Nicklaus or Tom Fazio. Indeed, the magazine's recent adoption of a "tradition" criterion is yet another way for its own editorial board to compensate for excess when its raters are swayed by modern glitz. And to preserve a place for walking, *Digest* assigns a modest number of bonus points depending upon whether the course allows walking on a restricted or unrestricted basis.

Golf is not without its own controversies. A number of its panelists are architect/designers, including Tom Doak, Pete and Alice Dye, Rees Jones, Robert Trent Jones, Jr., Jack Nicklaus, Arnold Palmer, Gary Player, Donald Steel, Tom Weiskopf, and Michael Wolveridge. What happens when professional rivalries begin influencing votes? To be sure, since Tom Doak started the list a decade ago it has moved from essentially the "Toughest golf courses" to a much more representative collection of the "Best golf courses." When panelists voted Doak's own layout, High Pointe in Michigan, as 97th in the country, a few cynics raised eyebrows. Doak, to his credit, offered to resign from overseeing the voting in order to preserve the credibility of the results, but editors at *Golf* refused to accept it and he continues to manage the balloting.

What's classical?

The Golden Age of Architecture is still golden. There is a remarkable consensus regarding the top-10. *Digest*'s elite in the country are: Pine Valley, followed by Cypress Point, Pebble Beach, Augusta National, Shinnecock Hills, Merion-East, Pinehurst #2, Oakmont, Crystal Downs in Michigan, and Winged Foot-West. *Golf*'s top-10 includes nine of these, with only The Country Club (Brookline, Massachusetts) displacing Crystal Downs. All of these courses predate 1935.

For what it's worth, when it comes to courses opened since 1965, *Digest* lists 34 on its poll while *Golf* lists 28. The difference has to do with *Golf* magazine raters seeing fewer modern courses and generally tending toward traditional designs.

Turnover in the ratings?

Quite a bit in the last generation. Consider the 1973 *Digest* list, when a good part of the rankings was still based on difficulty (i.e., yardage and course rating). Amazingly, Cypress Point was only grouped in the 41–50 category, Crystal Downs wasn't ranked at all, and the top-100 included such profoundly dull layouts as Concord in New York, International in Massachusetts, Doral-Blue in Florida, and Preston Trail in Texas. While the list was overwhelmingly East Coast-biased, it at least included such classic layouts as Bethpage Black and Fishers Island in New York and the University of New Mexico South Course. Nine of the courses ranked 1–50 in 1973 are no longer on the list today, while 27 of those ranked 51–100 have also been dropped.

Biggest problem with the ratings?

Too many fine layouts go unnoticed as raters tend to focus their attention on playing the top-100, as if collecting stamps as status symbols. There's also the accumulated effect of prestige, such as having hosted national major championships or being virtually inaccessible to the public, leading to a heightened sense of "preciousness" when it comes to raters evaluating these course. Many raters literally refuse to play a golf course unless it's a serious contender for top-100 ("why waste my time?"). Over 85 percent of these courses in the U.S are private and thus closed to the vast majority of golfers. To be sure, many of them are truly "great." But many are overrated just because they are famous, and the two (fame and greatness) have nothing to do with one another. Just because a course has hosted a major tournament doesn't endow it with the status of a great layout, though the mistake is often made.

Architecture and the Media

Whether in the form of books, magazines, videos, or television programming, media representations of golf are crucial to how we experience the game. Most fans know Pebble Beach intimately—before, and often without ever, having actually seen the course. So accustomed are we to televised tournament golf that the average player seems to emulate professionals when it comes to lining up putts or selecting a club. Green chairmen at country clubs regularly find themselves besieged by members who want their own courses to look as flawlessly manicured year-round as Augusta National looks one week a year on TV.

We need to be more sensitive to how golf courses are portrayed by the media. Golf scribes like Bernard Darwin and O.B. Keeler were thoroughly familiar with the game at every rank. If you surveyed the classical golf publications like *American Golfer* or *Golf Illustrated* from the 1920s, you'd find equal time devoted to amateur golf, women's golf, and the male professionals. The same was true of sports pages in American newspapers until the late 1940s.

That all changed with the advent of the glossy sports/golf magazines in the 1950s, followed by televised tournament coverage in the age of Arnold Palmer. The male professional tour came to dominate media attention; and with it, public perceptions of the game. Moreover, the look of articles changed dramatically. Text shrank. Visual imagery came to predominate. And the trend continues today. In journalism they call it "Macnews." Articles today are much shorter than they were 20 years ago. Impressive photography has tended to crowd out analysis. Instead of thoughtful reviews, we're down to numerical rankings.

When golf courses are discussed, the narrative voice is not that of your average player but that of a (male) power golfer who regularly contemplates reaching 500-yard par-fives in two. Only for such a golfer can a 390-yard hole be described as a "short par-four."

The trend is particularly American. Consider such a basic text as *The World Atlas of Golf*. When the Briton, Pat Ward-Thomas, or his Australian counterpart, Peter Thomson, describe some of the world's legendary courses, they adopt the perspective of an average player out for an encounter with lovingly fashioned land. The emphasis is on the feel and texture of the terrain. Now turn to the pages written by American writer, (the late) Charles Price. A supremely knowledgeable scribe, he describes his native courses with the help of superlatives proclaiming this hole being the "best" and that one being the "toughest." And all of a sudden, numbers do the work of words, as if accounts of Palmer beating a 452-yard hole into submission with a drive and seven-iron have anything to do with the game most golfers actually experience.

An accepted practice of serious criticism already exists in such art forms as food, sculpture, cinema, and music. Why shouldn't there be the same tradition in golf course design? Historically, criticism does not mean complaining or condemning. It means to educate an audience and to explore ways of improving upon an art form. The assumption here is that thoughtful, discriminating writing helps make for a better game.

There are many in the golf industry today who think that the function of the media is crassly to promote the game. Advertisers, after all, pay considerable sums of money for precisely that purpose. There's at least one glossy magazine out there whose pages are literally for sale to anyone who wants to pay for what amounts to an unannounced advertorial.

For writers and journalists on the editorial side, however, there are different ways of fulfilling their responsibility to the public. How credible is it, for instance, to read one glowing review after another? Doesn't it make for more credible journalism to confront a serious and sustained analysis that raises questions and peers behind the hype? That, after all, is what investigative journalism has long been about.

There's every reason to believe that when it comes to golf course criticism, the public would be better served if more writers and TV commentators explored the subtlety and beauty of sound architecture rather than simply hawking a new layout as somebody's latest and greatest "signature design." A few fragile egos might get bruised along the way. But the game as a whole would benefit.

6

Read Any Good Greens Lately?

The First Two Inches of Break
Are Inside the Cup

For years, golfers have been asking me of what use is the study of golf course architecture to their game. The assumption is that if the knowledge can't be applied to improve your game, then it has no intrinsic value. I've always been uncomfortable with such a view, especially because the art of golf course design is such an inspiring subject—part of our cultivation as sports enthusiasts with more sophisticated tastes than, say, bowlers, footballers, or students of roller derby.

Admittedly, though, the question has nagged at me for years. Every golfer, after all, yearns to improve. Many spend thousands of dollars in the (vain) pursuit. Indeed, some golf magazines that used to run articles to read have now been reduced to offering nothing but a series of cartoons promising you all manner of sure-fire tips.

It's time to sneak an instructional piece in. Admittedly, struggling 13-handicappers like this writer are not usually considered reliable sources of help. But what follows is the simplest, most compelling piece of advice possible, and all of it built upon a vast repertoire of knowledge from the annals of course design.

Here it is. When lining up to putt, especially on shorter putts, calculate the break from the center of the cup, not the edge.

I have tried this piece of advice on talented golfers with 20 years of experience and they've looked upon me with amazement. And a desperate feeling of "How stupid could I have been all those years?" Maybe that was Tom Watson's problem during his long dry spell, which only ended in 1996. For too long, he has been just missing it on the edge from what should have been easily makeable range.

The thinking behind this tip is simple. The golf hole is the only aspect of the entire course whose specifications are standardized in the rules of golf: 4 and 1/4 inches in diameter. Now, think of yourself lining up a five foot putt. You see three inches of break, aim three inches outside the edge, and put a perfect stroke on it. What happens? You've missed it by two inches. How often do golfers complain about overreading putts? Now we know why.

The answer is simple. They're not misreading the putt; nor, for that matter, mis-hitting it. Rather, the mistake is more elemental. They are miscalculating the point from which the break ought to be measured. If you calculate that three inch putt from the center of the hole and not the edge, then you'll be aiming only one inch off the hole!

Golf is hard enough. Why handicap yourself further by forgetting that the first two inches of every break occurs within the radius of the hole? Figure break off the center, not the edge, and you're likely to make a bundle more of those short putts you've been missing. The bet here is that a frightening number of players, good and bad alike, have never perceived something so simple.

Modern Greens Construction Demands Craftsmanship

It's enough trouble just keeping the front lawn from dying. Imagine the difficulty of preparing ground so that it will yield turf appropriate for putting. Every golfer who has ever criticized the conditions of greens ought to spend some time learning how the things are built. Some time ago I spent a few days on Kiawah Island in South Carolina, watching Pete Dye and his construction supervisor, Jason McCoy, at work on the seaside course as they prepped it for the 1991 Ryder Cup matches.

When criticized that his courses look artificial, Pete concedes that "truer words have never been spoken." What else can a golf course be but a contrivance of man and machine? At Kiawah Island he and his crew of 110 moved hundreds of thousands of cubic yards of dirt and created a playing surface some eight to twelve feet above its "natural" level. Water trucks and various jeeps scurried for months along the service road surrounding the plateau. Small wonder that from afar the course looks like a monstrous irradiated souffle that had escaped a madman's kitchen.

Pete and chief features shaper Tom Simpson are over at a green, shooting levels. They set up the transit and take readings through the lens. The conventional method is to read the levels off of premarked grading rods placed at numerous points on the green.

Modern greens are built to about a two percent grade, meaning an elevation change of two feet vertically for every 100 feet laterally. In laying out a putting surface, that translates into 2.4 inches per ten feet of length.

Every green has to have a certain number of "pinnable" areas some 10–15 feet across, each with no more than that two percent slope. Swales can be more severe, but the greater the slope around pinnable areas, the larger those relatively level zones will need to be. When older style, steeply sloped greens are mowed down to modern standards—Stimpmeter readings of eight or more—they simply become unputtable. The old 17th green at Inverness in Toledo averaged a six percent slope and so had to be rebuilt. Winged Foot today averages close to three percent and borders on the extreme.

Slopes are built into fairways as well. Without a two percent slope on fairway surfaces, water will pool up rather than drain off. Feature shapers, the folks who run bulldozers and who "massage" the dirt into finished shape, can usually "eyeball" acceptable slope grades in landing areas, though an occasional checkup with a level is necessary.

Construction specifications set out by the USGA call for the green to be subgraded to a depth of 18 inches below the final playing level. When this preliminary excavation has been made, Tom—or sometimes Pete himself—will climb aboard a little Jacobsen Smithco with a manual drag rake and make last minute adjustments.

Then a mechanical trencher is brought in to cut drainage beds eight inches deep into the subgrade. Into this they lay a two-inch layer of pea gravel (1/4" to 3/8" size), followed by four-inch diameter perforated drainpipe, then a two-inch covering layer of more pea gravel so that the trench is filled up to the subgrade. Next, a four-inch layer of more pea gravel over the whole surface. Then, they layer in two inches of coarse sand (1- to 2-mm particles) followed by 12 inches of root mix (85% sand, 15% *Sphagum* Canadian peat moss).

A final fling with the drag rake is now needed to complete the surface. Afterward, the green is fumigated with methyl bromide. Add Bermuda grass seed, lots of water, wait around a few weeks, and then putt.

A year after all of this, it was time for the Ryder Cup, and the greens at Kiawah Island looked and rolled as slick as glass. Few onlookers, indeed, few of the competitors, will ever care how the greens were built. But if proper care weren't being taken on the putting surfaces now, problems would eventually show up.

When it comes to obtaining solid putting surfaces, proper maintenance down the road requires painstaking construction at the outset.

Riviera's Greens: An Autopsy

One question dominated conversation among PGA Tour players at the 1996 Nissan Open at Riviera Country Club in Los Angeles: What kind of shape are the greens in? The answer was not bad—at least when compared with their condition six months earlier, when Riviera hosted the PGA Championship. Their deplorable shape that infamous week in August 1995 resulted in criticism, embarrassment, and controversy at one of America's most distinguished architectural gems.

The putting surfaces, which were totally rebuilt in 1993, became an object of industry-wide concern, the more so since the course went on to host three tournaments within the space of 13 months: the Nissan Open in February 1995, the PGA in August, and another Nissan Open in March 1996.

What went wrong with the rebuilding process? How can it be avoided in the future?

The Riviera project was undertaken with the best of intentions: to improve the greens in time for the 1995 PGA Championship. The man brought in to oversee the project, Ben Crenshaw, is a two-time Masters champion. He has long enjoyed impeccable credentials as a lover of classical courses, and knew how to undertake such a sensitive restoration. Establishing turf on putting surfaces can be delicate, however, especially when there are powerful time constraints dictated by the scheduling of PGA Tour events and a major championship.

The result has proved embarrassing, and to this day questions remain. What exactly happened? And what lessons can clubs learn from the controversial events that ensued?

One thing is certain; many people have suffered. Some have been targeted for criticism—largely unfairly, as it turns out, but such is the nature of public scrutiny of high-profile projects. Mr. Noboru Watanabe, the Japanese industrialist from the Marukin Corporation, paid $108 million for the course in 1989, spent another $2 million in search of better greens, and now finds himself with a devalued product. Ben Crenshaw also has been affected, not only because he (and design associate Bill Coore) toiled so hard on-site but also because the grass that didn't quite take root bears his name.

Most of all, the membership has suffered. For two and a half years it has been dealing with bulldozers, consultants' reports, less than ideal putting surfaces, and finger pointing.

It seems to have become open season on Riviera, particularly among press pundits too busy typing to undertake sustained research. The club first became the object of unkind and unfair nationalist rhetoric when Mr. Watanabe bought it from the Hathaway family for what was widely acknowledged to be well above market value.

Then came former Riviera member O.J. Simpson and more sensationalist boulevard press than anyone could have imagined. "Enquiring minds" rang Riviera's phones off the hook in search of more lurid news, contributing to a circus-like atmosphere that bore no relation to the club's long and glorious tradition.

And then there was the 1995 PGA Championship, a debacle if there ever was one. Too few spectators turned out for a major tournament in which the greens rolled over and died in midstream. The greens looked blue—or was it purple and crusty?—that week. In either case, they became a laughingstock, a greenkeeper's worst nightmare, and a reminder of how complex it is to rebuild putting surfaces.

Riviera dates back to 1926, when George Thomas was asked by the Los Angeles Athletic Club to build a magnificent facility 20 miles northwest of downtown. For decades, the golf course successfully hosted national tournaments, including numerous L.A. Opens, the 1948 U.S. Open, and the 1983 PGA. Classical greens, a mix of sandy loam with a minimum of drain tile, have held up well on many golf courses, even under the demands of modern green speeds. But Riviera draws an exceptionally high level of play. By the late 1980s, 60,000 rounds were played annually on greens that averaged only 4,300 sq.ft.; small by today's standards. "You get a golf course like that has medium to small greens and they play all those rounds, and it had better have strong turf," Crenshaw said.

Several factors compounded the stress. One was that acceptable areas for pin placements were gradually being reduced. Years of sand accumulation from greenside bunkers that had been built close to the putting surfaces created new contours that gradually shrank the usable cupping area of each green.

Second, as the premier club in the area and as annual host of the L.A. Open, Riviera was expected always to be in peak shape. A steady stream of guest play and corporate outings attested to such lofty expectations. The excessive demands of trying to achieve tournament-quality greens year-round created a whole catalog of turf maintenance problems.

In August 1991 and again in August 1992, Riviera's greens nearly died because of poor drainage, heavy play, warm weather, and fungus problems. A decision was made in late 1992 to "core out" and rebuild the putting surfaces. Crenshaw and Coore were selected to oversee the restoration of the contours and greenside bunkers. Ed Connor of Golforms Inc. of Florida, was hired to record the contours and recreate them on the new greens. He was also responsible for construction of the subsurface drainage system.

Some time before the project commenced, interim general manager Yasushi "Joe" Masaki decided to use washed sod—turf that has had all soil washed away from the roots, leaving them bare for replanting—instead of seeding the new greens. Crenshaw and Coore implored them not to sod the greens, but the club's front office wanted people back on the course as soon as possible, and washed sod appeared to be the answer.

Following the advice of nationally renowned soil consultant Dick Psolla, the club chose an aggressive-growing Crenshaw/Cato blend grass, with the soil a modified U.S.Golf Association-recommended mix comprising 80 percent sand, 15 percent Canadian peat, and 5 percent Dakota peat by volume.

After the 1993 L.A. Open, the club began building 18 alternate Bermuda grass greens; the real greens were to be torn up and rebuilt in phases of six, with the first group scheduled for sodding in late June that year. The first green to be done, No. 10, was sodded in mid-July, completed just in time for the filming of "Chrysler's Best 18 Holes in America" (featuring John

Daly, Tom Kite, Davis Love III, and Fuzzy Zoeller). That green, at 2,400 sq.ft. the smallest on the course, has since proved to be Riviera's worst. The next five greens all were sodded six weeks behind schedule.

Why the delay? Work had to be postponed because the club was delayed in securing the proper permits in what turned out to be an unusually complex bureaucratic maze. Riviera sits in a flood plain, and the introduction of 8,000 tons of soil materials required governmental approvals. Moreover, hauling it in at 60 tons of materials a trailer load also required permission for the 130 truck trips needed through the upscale Brentwood neighborhood.

The delays had a subtle but decisive effect on the condition of the sod, intended to be placed on the new greens mix in midsummer. Delays pushed the date of sodding back, and by the time the sod was harvested for Riviera at West Coast Turf, a nursery in California, it was, says Psolla, "a little on the mature side. Less than one year old is ideal; longer, and there is more thatch and root mass."

The basic strength of the Crenshaw/Cato Bent was its dense root mass and aggressive growth. But even when properly washed of soil, and there is every indication that this batch was indeed properly washed, the overmaturity meant that it would have developed a thicker root mass than preferred. Aggressive verticutting (breaking up root mass to promote downward growth) and aerifying could usually handle such conditions, but that would create some additional stress by imposing layers of sand upon the new turf.

Further complicating matters was the shortened growing season. With Riviera's greens surrounded by towering eucalyptus trees, and the course sitting in a canyon bed, the turf had enough trouble getting proper air circulation and sunlight. Because of the late sodding, growth was taking place in September and October, with even less sunlight. Looming ahead in February 1994 was another L.A. Open. Some members pressed management to surrender the tournament for one season, but the front office held to its contract.

Soon after the greens were sodded, major troubles appeared. The greens started losing grass on the surface and drainage was poor. The greens went into shock every time they were aerified, even though aerification was necessary to help establish some root structure. Lack of rain in the winter of 1994 hurt, as did some cold weather. As Connor says about turf growth, "Whatever you go into October with is what you come out with in the spring."

The result in 1994 was greens that were not ready for the L.A. Open. In June, superintendent Jim McPhilomy resigned after a disagreement with newly hired consultant and turf expert, Bill Bengeyfield, a former USGA employee who had been brought in by new general manager Peter Pino to get the course ready for the 1995 L.A. Open and PGA Championship. Former club manager Masaki, meanwhile, became comptroller, and also continued serving as vice president for Marukin Corp.

In August of 1994, Riviera hired former La Quinta CC greenkeeper Bill Baker after a nationwide search. Baker made good progress with the greens and protected them during the 1995 L.A. Open by not cutting them too low.

Still, the root structure was never where it should have been: no more than three inches, when it should have seven or eight. The basic agronomic problem was a dense layer of thatch that had built up under the sod. The roots, instead of penetrating the greens mix, had grown out, or up, and so were never fully established. Water drained poorly, not because of problems with the greens mix, rather because the water never penetrated the thick blanket of thatch. As Psolla explains it, the problem wasn't with the percolation rate of the soil, it was with the poor infiltration of the thatch that wouldn't allow water through.

Two months before the PGA, Monday corporate outings and charity events were discontinued, and then the course was closed for five days before the tournament. That week, the greens measured about 8 on the Stimpmeter. That's when superintendent Baker found himself under pressure from PGA of America senior director of tournaments Kerry Haigh to speed up the putting surfaces.

According to Norman Klaparda, a Riviera member who served as green chairman during the PGA, Baker reluctantly agreed to top-dress the greens and then on Wednesday of the tournament to "pump up the fertilizer application. Within 24 hours, the game was over."

Another prominent Riviera member, tournament chairman Dick Caruso, recalls a conversation that week among himself, Baker, Haigh, and Jim Magnusson (a PGA staff member and 1995 tournament director) concerning who had the final say when it came to getting the course in tournament shape. Caruso said that Haigh responded: "I'll assume the blame for it."

By Sunday afternoon before the first practice round, the greens were showing extreme stress. They had began to turn brown and the topdressing appeared to burn them. By late Monday afternoon, they were clearly dying. So the greens were given a light fertilizing to bolster their appearance. This backfired, because not enough water could be put on the greens and still keep them firm for the tournament. The fertilizing was repeated after Wednesday's practice round, resulting in a complete burning of the greens, which was evident on television.

Within hours after the final putt by winner Steve Elkington, Riviera's management met and called in Bengeyfield to take control of the greens. He outlined a plan that differed from what Baker wanted to do. In September 1995, the club held a green committee meeting at which more than 100 members voiced their concerns.

This is a membership that has been dutifully paying $426 monthly fees without being able to enjoy the full extent of the golf course. Between 1990 and 1995, initiation fees increased from $15,000 to $75,000. The members secured their own independent consultant, for which the club footed the bill.

He was Billy Fuller, former Augusta National Golf Club superintendent, and the soil work was done by Chuck Dixon of Dixon Labs. Fuller recommended that management come up with a contingency plan if the current greens could not be saved. He confirmed that there was a one-inch layer under the grass that was preventing proper drainage.

Meanwhile, Bill Baker "resigned" as superintendent November 30, 1995—not entirely voluntarily. Bengeyfield has since been serving as the club's acting superintendent from his Idaho home, making visits about once every three weeks and coordinating work with newly appointed superintendent Dan Vaquez—formerly Baker's assistant, and now the fifth superintendent at Riviera since Watanabe bought the club in 1989.

Through all of this, the membership has remained supportive of Watanabe. The real tension is between the members, represented on the Board of Governors, and the front office people. In November 1995, USGA President David Fay visited Riviera to evaluate it for the 1998 U.S. Senior Open which is scheduled there. Among the issues to be determined is the extent to which Riviera members would volunteer their services. Many of them remain alienated in the aftermath of their experience with the 1995 PGA.

For now, outside play has been reduced marginally, though the course will still log some 60,000 rounds this year. The club has taken steps to ensure the integrity of the 10th green by building an alternate putting surface, to be used sparingly in order to relieve traffic. Crenshaw turned down the assignment. It was successfully handled by Ron Forse, a Pittsburgh-based designer with a reputation as one of the country's restoration geniuses.

And the greens themselves? They appear to be responding to intensive aerification. It has helped, too, that since Baker's departure the greens have been watered much less. The roots are making marginal progress, and the thatch zone appears to be thinning. Progress through 1996 has been slow and it will take at least several years for the greens to fully recover. Or will it turn out that this is simply a Band-Aid, a measure to keep dysfunctional greens on life support? If that's the case, then Riviera might have to strip off the sod, clean out the thatch, and seed, not sod, a whole new set of greens. For now, Riviera and its members are working to make up for a process gone awry.

There remains much in-house debate, some of it deeply embittered. Who, after all, can blame folks for feeling passionate about their home course? There are surely certain lessons to be drawn from this. For one, the importance of comprehensive planning, and secondly, acknowledging when mistakes were made rather than patching things up and running away from problems. There are also serious issues regarding the responsibility of tournament associations to the venues where they are, after all, guests. And then there's the small matter of money, of the pressures exerted from within to generate revenue when the health of a golf course is at stake.

☙

Brown, Not Green, Is Better

Golf course superintendents have come a long way over the years in terms of professional training and skills. Greenkeepers, once little more than an afterthought to golf, have now become integral. No small part of that is due to efforts of the Golf Course Superintendents Association of America on behalf of its 16,000 members.

At every golf course, whether public, private, or resort, superintendents enter into complex negotiations with members, club managers, and green chairmen. Invariably, the object of these discussions is course conditioning: how to keep the course as green as possible, and how, at the same time, to pay for it.

Actually, the toughest part of a superintendent's job is not turf management but the politics of his position. So stressful is this aspect of the job that in Florida, where the demands are probably greater than anywhere else in the country, the average tenure of a superintendent at any one club is only five years.

Where does the demand for the all-green golf course come from? Ten times out of ten, from the membership. For a variety of reasons, the bug has been implanted in the minds of millions of golfers that lush and plush make for better golf.

Perhaps television has had the greatest influence on this perception. Network television cover—in full color, no less—of golf tournaments in winter and early spring might well have made the initial difference. The sight of a perfectly manicured golf course like Augusta National, with its grand plazas of fairways and greens, must have been revolutionary. Through the mid-1960s, most golf courses were watered manually rather than by automatically controlled sprinklers. The advent of new irrigation technology and newfound knowledge in turfgrass research has enabled the image of the all-green course to take hold.

Nowadays, players look down the road at some heavily budgeted private club and assume that their own semiprivate course can also have perfect turf. Or players have traveled to a resort down south, and come back up north wondering why on April 15 their home course has yet to drain.

Yet such thinking overlooks basic operating factors that lead to marked variance in conditioning from one club to the next: how the course was initially constructed; its soil characteristics; its drainage; the local climate; and the funds made available by the greens committee.

The secret of many a superintendent is to allow the golf course a little slack and to let brown take over where green once was. If more golf courses pursued such a policy, we would save on water, labor costs, and environmental risk, and at the same time make the game more enjoyable for the great majority of golfers.

In northern climates, bent grass now predominates. Beginning some 45 years ago, blue- and ryegrasses were replaced by bents that could be cut lower, allowing the ball to sit up better. The result was a dramatic increase in the water requirements and maintenance regimens required to keep bent grass green throughout the season. But the constant watering made the all-bent courses play longer and slower.

Golf courses today could offer fine playing surfaces if members decided to cut back on watering and seeded for more ryegrasses. And there's no reason why rough areas need to be watered at all. Here, native fescues with their brownish, tawny color can be encouraged to grow. This thin, narrow-blade turf is drought-resistant and beautiful to look at. The result would be added color and texture, a faster golf course, and a reemphasis upon the ground game, all the while saving on water and pesticides.

In warmer regions, where Bermuda grass prevails, superintendents are often required to manage an arduous procedure of transition by which tees, fairways, and greens are overseeded with ryes and bents to come through in time for the winter season. Bermuda, it turns out, does not hold up well when nighttime temperatures dip under about 50°. If Bermuda goes dormant, it turns a kind of light brown and thins out. Not terribly good for putting, but there's nothing wrong with it for fairways and tees. Yet resorts and private clubs spend a fortune in that delicate transition process because tourists and club members persist in their demands for an all-green golf course year-round.

Lower budget courses in the South avoid such transitional overseeding, as do a number of desert courses, where the water requirements are severe. If more golf courses restricted their transition zones to their greens only, we would have courses that were more interesting to look at and play.

A drier, browner golf course would allow the ball to roll farther. A faster course would work to the advantage of women, senior golfers, and all those who tend to hit the ball relatively low. It would increase their distance by increasing the amount of roll they got.

Architects today encourage the aerial game over the ground game. Greens and fairways are more tightly bunkered than ever. Forced carries over water and sand are now commonplace, whereas 50 years ago they were frowned upon, and the rule was to give people a bail-out area to which they could play safe and run the ball.

A return to browner values would restore the impetus for more creative course design and enable architects to reclaim classical strategic principles. It would also take the pressure off superintendents. Their job is tough enough without also having to keep every blade of grass green the year-round.

7

In the Beginning There Was Sand

Mysteries of the 14th
at St. Andrews

The first time Bobby Jones competed on the Old Course at St. Andrews in 1921, he tore up his scorecard at the 11th hole—in the middle of competition—and vowed never to return. But he did come back, won both the British Open and the Amateur there and later acclaimed it as the course he would gladly choose were he confined to play only one.

The Old Course stands out for the naturalness of the golf strategy it calls for. Its sand-strewn features and crazily bunkered greens reveal themselves gradually to the patient golfer as a classic test of golf. Here is a course with only 11 greens; with fairways 100 yards wide; where you can hit the ball dead left off the tee all day and always have a clear shot into the green; and with not a tree to orient you along the way. An architect who built such a layout today would be sued for gross incompetence. The first time you scan this barren, windswept moonscape you think you've been hoodwinked; the victim of a cosmic joke. Yet only those who have walked its fairways a dozen times can know how compelling are its mysteries.

The 14th hole, Long Hole, is a par-five of medium length, 523 yards, bordered along the entire right side by a stone wall marking out-of-bounds. A group of nasty traps, "the Beardies," will swallow a tee shot hit too far left. But a drive down the center lands you in "Elysian Fields," a lush plateau of fairway that seems strangely removed from the hillocks and bunkered mayhem so characteristic of the Old Course.

A solid drive will take you past the Beardies and beyond the small breach in the wall. Just above the putting surface, emerging from the far end of the course, rises the medieval town of St. Andrews. From Elysian Fields the Old Course first displays itself as the center of a tiny sovereignty devoted entirely to golf. From here you have your first clear view of the town which nurtured the game.

Red brick and grey stone buildings frame the final fairway. Behind the 18th green sits a little park, the most popular rendezvous point in town. Off to the right you can survey the campus of St. Andrews University, and as your eyes sweep left you see the whole town, and further left, the North Sea itself. A fifteenth-century cathedral presides over the town, its presence truly a blessing. This church offers more than religious refuge; its steeple provides a reference point for golfers who might otherwise face blind shots on holes 14, 15, and 17.

Some years ago I caddied for an American during his first tour of St. Andrews. My player, a near scratch-golfer, came to the 14th a mere handful of shots over par. After a good drive of some 240 yards to the middle of Elysian Fields he turned to me for advice. An uncommonly mild wind blew in our faces. He could see the red flag clearly, though not the putting surface, and thought he should have a go at it.

When a caddie's salary reaches the $25-per-round bracket he does not make light of his work. "Sir," I told him, "there's 'Hell' up ahead. A career three-wood won't carry it. Better to play around it."

"Hell" is a hideous gaping wound in the land about 80 yards short of the green. Technically you would call it a bunker, but this is no mere sand hazard. Perhaps some primitive land mine from ancient wars with the English had gouged out this pit 12 feet deep and some 20 yards across. From its walls protruded a coarse, sickly brown grass in which, legend has it, one can still find gutta-percha balls.

Two hundred and ten yards to clear this mid-fairway crater. I knew he had no chance of carrying it, and I began plotting safer alternatives.

A low-handicap golfer does not travel 3,500 miles and expend goodness knows how much money in order to play safe on par-fives. For these reasons I ruled out the route normally taken by cautious players at the Long Hole: a second shot with an iron designed to keep the ball just above Hell for a clear third shot to the green below. My golfer would rightly have been insulted had I suggested such a timid path. But instead of acquiescing in his desire to use a fairway wood, I turned 30° to the left, pointed to an area in front of the adjacent 5th tee, and suggested he hit a three-iron there.

He looked at me as if I were crazy; as if I had not the slightest idea what golf was all about. He was intent, I could see, upon hitting the three-wood. There are those moments in caddying when you've spoken your piece and you just have to stand there and watch your man bloody himself. This was going to be one of those times. I tried hard not to be smug about it.

The ball jumped off the clubface and screamed skyward like a missile targeted at the green. It hung high for a long time before descending slowly, very slowly, smack into the middle of Hell. He turned to me without a word and simply held out his hand. I fumbled for the bottom pocket and managed to find another pellet. After handing it to him I quietly pointed to his three-iron. This time he followed my advice "just for the heck of it." With seeming indifference he hit his Mulligan shot precisely where I had suggested—down the fifth fairway.

After this shot he picked the pitching wedge from his golf bag. He instructed me to wait in the adjoining fairway by his ball while he hit out from the infernal bunker. After watching him leap into the hazard I lit up a cigarette and waited. Too bad, I said to myself, I had not brought along a cigar.

All of the well-visited bunkers at St. Andrews have names: Road Bunker, Cheape's, Coffin. But none of them allows you to play in such privacy as the one in which my player now found himself. What exactly transpired down there I can only guess. Only after several minutes did there appear signs of life. A golf club flew out of the bunker as if it were a broken helicopter blade. A few seconds later I saw the top of his head. It bobbed somewhat, rose for an instant, his arms went up, and then he disappeared from view, only to reemerge, this time in the clear. My player had finally managed to extricate himself. In his left hand he held a golf ball.

Time now to play the Mulligan. From his position in the 5th fairway he could approach the 14th green not from head-on but from an angle of nearly 45°. The green, 130 yards distant, sloped sharply away, and the highest point of the whole putting surface was the front right edge. Sheepish players who have layed up short of Hell face an impossible approach from the regular fairway because there's no way to hold the green. But from the adjoining fairway the hole opens up somewhat and you can at least see part of the putting surface.

Golfers in America do not often confront greens sloping away from the line of play. At St. Andrews they are nearly the rule. The green at the 14th was shaped, or simply developed over time, to accommodate play from both directions. Only by understanding the genesis of the links does it make sense to play such a putting surface: a green better suited to play from the other side.

Nobody built the Old Course. It is not the product of civil engineers who orchestrated their construction according to blueprints. The golfing gods themselves allowed these links slowly to emerge upon sandy soil that during past millennia had lain under water. It was on this linksland many centuries ago that human beings began regularly to chase around a little ball in order to hit it again with a stick.

Under King James IV of Scotland, a parliamentary decree in 1491 warned the townsmen of St. Andrews not to while away their time playing golf. With the ever-present threat of invasion from England, citizens were instructed to dispense with their clubs and to practice archery instead. The edict was promptly ignored. Two and a half centuries later the once-independent Scottish kingdom succumbed to English armies.

Meanwhile, the game of golf flourished. Along the beach of St. Andrews, men accustomed themselves to playing a route of seven holes that ran in more or less a line from near town center toward the River Eden. One day, the date of which no one knows, people began playing back from the opposite direction to the holes they had played when going "out." At one point, there were 22 holes, but the ones near the town and the clubhouse were deemed too short, and by the late eighteenth century the number of holes had been reduced to 18. Gradually, enormous double putting surfaces developed to absorb play in both directions. To prevent confusion, the outward holes were graced with white flags, the inward holes with flags of red. At the last green, however, the flag reverted to white, lest players be unable to discern it against the backdrop of the reddish building behind the park.

Through a process of natural erosion, sand left behind when the North Sea receded was continually shaped and reshaped. Constant winds and driving rain helped create the very largest bunkers and mounds which came to dot the course. In hollowed-out areas and along the leeward side of mounds, sheep would find shelter from the weather. No grass could grow on these trampled-down areas. Much later, after golf began, places to which golfers habitually hit their shots became ground down from divots and gouges. In this strange concatenation of nature and human habit, the Old Course acquired its bunkers and mounds, and later, its fairways and greens.

Play on the Old Course normally proceeds down the right side of the double fairways and to the right half of each double green. This pattern only changes on the four short holes at the far end of the course, the "loop" holes, 8 through 11. Here golfers aim for the left side of shared fairways and greens.

Old-timers at St. Andrews refer to this traditional routing as the "right-handed" course. But several greens, the 14th among them, are pitched severely away from this "normal" line of play. On these holes, the 12th say, fairway bunkers only 50 yards off the tee serve no apparent purpose. But if you use some imagination and construe the golf course in reverse, then suddenly these features assume importance. They are part of another layout. You can actually play the entire track backward! They call it the "left-handed" course.

This "left-handed" course used to be part of a regular rotation at St. Andrews well into the twentieth century. One year, when the British Amateur was slated for St. Andrews, the greenkeeper saw that the calendar called for the "left-handed" course" that week and so the championship was played accordingly.

From a makeshift tee before the 18th green, golfers would

play down the left side of the fairway to the 17th green. Then from the 17th green, play would proceed to the left side of the next double green, as if approaching No. 16 from behind. This second "left-hand" hole, by the way, demands a perfectly placed drive and a second shot around the corner of the Old Course Hotel: an approach more difficult than the famous drive off the regular 17th tee over the hotel parking lot. By continuing in this "left-handed" manner you can play the entire Old Course in reverse. And when you come upon the 14th green, this time from the 15th fairway, you will find a putting surface pitched neatly in your direction.

I condensed this geographical history for my player that afternoon as he prepared to approach the 14th green. From this side, of course, no lob shot would hold. A ball flown to the pin would bound over into a bunker or heavy grass. His repertoire of full-bore golf shots would prove useless. And after all those hours on the driving range back home, smacking away at buckets of balls in reverie of conquering St. Andrews!

From the left side of the fairway, though, the green opened up just slightly. He had room to work the ball. A bump-and-run shot, hit into the mound, would allow the ball to hold the green. After consulting with me he decided to improvise with a punched-down five-iron. The ball carried only about 80 yards and then bounded and rolled toward the flag. It came to rest pin-high, 20 feet from the cup.

After watching to make sure the ball stayed in place, he walked slowly, silently, to the green. Was he basking in the glory of his new-found knowledge? Perhaps, I hoped, he had learned what it really meant to play golf shots at St. Andrews.

It would take much time for him to learn all the other shots that this eerie links demands. Only through patience does one learn the Old Course, for the mystery of golf at St. Andrews resides in the presence and weight of its history. You begin to see it in every shot. You feel it in all the bunkers with names and in the town where golf was born. No other golf course, however well-designed, can emulate this enduring past. And no first encounter with its mysteries can exhaust what St. Andrews has to offer.

The Linksland of Machrihanish

The water, the wind, the sounds of the open sea—these are some of the elements that define linksland golf and make it an experience unlike any other in the game. Add firm, sandy soil, throw in bunkers that appear to have been placed by a madman, and then place the pins on putting surfaces that look like oversized potato chips. A rainstorm getting in the way of your backswing? As the Scots say, if you don't like the weather along the shore, just wait a half hour, it will likely change.

Everything has its natural place on the links, even a green placed just beyond a stone wall, or a public footpath crossing the middle of the first and last fairways. Look out upon the golf course and you'll see thick stands of heather and gorse but no trees. Seedlings could scarcely take root in the howling winds. The result, still seen today at such pure links as Dornoch, Montrose, or Western Gailes, strikes many golfers as the strangest feature of all about classical links. The holes have the appearance of land shaved all the way down. There is no vertical dimension against which to judge any of the holes.

In Scotland, golf is a ground game, not an aerial game. The firmer soil allows unlimited possibilities for low-slung shots. Moreover, the sandier seaside soil drains much better than inland clay and so will accommodate deeper bunkers and swales. The result is a magical array of hummocks and rolls that, when viewed with the sun low to the horizon, conveys the play of rippling shadows. With all their texture, color, and form, seaside courses look stunningly natural. Their complex form is something no human handicraft can emulate.

Pure linksland lends itself to solid golfing turf like no other naturally occurring soil. It has proved uniquely receptive to hybrid grasses—a guarantee against blight wiping out any one plant species. Those grasses that took hold spread long thin roots that anchored in the sand. They needed little water to thrive. These are the forebears of what today are called "fescues." As for fertilizer, the seaweed washed up on shore or left behind as the sea receded proved a rich source of vital nutrients. Small wonder today that many British and Irish greenskeepers use a home-bred compound of rotting seaweed, blood, and iron. Greenkeeping was simpler in a pre-pesticide world.

Open shoreline also welcomes variety. Grass textures proliferate, as hybrid turf flourishes. All manner of habitat finds sustenance on this ground. By day, ospreys and gulls hover overhead; at night, the fairways come literally alive as rabbits emerge from their hideouts.

The call of the linksland has beckoned players for centuries. Nothing in the game exercises a more powerful attraction than golf where sand meets the sea.

Technically, "links" refers to the sandy soil that has been left behind by receding open seas. Golfers in the fifteenth and sixteenth centuries took to playing their newfound skills upon these naturally suited seaside venues. They, in turn, made their own mark upon the land. In such cases, greenkeepers reluctantly abandoned their efforts at cultivating grass and conceded instead to complete the bunkers that had inadvertently been in the works.

One peculiar dimension of Scottish linksland courses is that often, the sea has receded so far from the golfing grounds that the water no longer is a factor. This is the case at Royal Troon, St. Andrews, and Muirfield and at all the English sites for the British Open. There are, however, courses where the shoreline literally laps the course and brings the seas directly into play. Perhaps the most dramatic example of this is at one of the least known yet best reputed of all true links courses: Machrihanish Golf Club, near Campbeltown, at the southern end of Scotland's Kintyre Peninsula.

The golf course is 40 miles due west of Troon, but the only overland route there is by the road through Argyll and then down the length of Kintyre—a trip of some 160 miles. It's possible to take a short-hop charter plane over the water, but the drive is much more intriguing as the Kintyre Peninsula contains some of Scotland's loveliest roads.

The course sits upon Machrihanish Bay, at the point where

the North Channel opens onto the Atlantic Ocean. From the farthest reaches of the course, a golfer blessed with momentary fair weather can gaze out to sea and view both Northern Ireland and the Lower Hebridean Islands.

The links at Machrihanish were founded on March 20, 1876, when a committee of five laid out a 10-hole course. Three years later, Old Tom Morris expanded the course to 18 holes. The course assumed its present guise in 1914, when J.H. Taylor, a distinguished Open Champion, rebuilt Machrihanish. During World War II, the Royal Air Force requisitioned a piece of the golf courses for an air base. After the war, Sir Guy Campbell built three new holes and substantially revised the other 15. Today, the 6,228 yard course plays to par 70. As with all classical linksland courses, however, the story is neither distance nor par. On land so exposed to the elements as lower Kintyre Peninsula, the winds, prevailing from the west, bring all that a golfer can bear to handle. Sometimes, much more.

The opening tee shot establishes Machrihanish's character. "Battery," a 423-yard hole, turns gracefully left, requiring a drive over the inlet of a beach. A modest opening salvo needs only to bite off part of the beach. The ambitious golfer, however, will have to carry the greater part of beachfront property.

From then on it is a lovely walk among rolling sand hills covered with coarse grasses. Fairways and greens seem to tumble with the dunesland. At seven, "Bruach More," the second shot has to carry a massive sand bunker cut deep into the face of a mound looming over the right corner of the dogleg. The RAF installation stands guard at the turn; the constant to and fro of aircraft a discordant reminder that this golf course can never be quite as otherworldly as its harsh, austere beauty deserves.

Host professional Gavin Crockett proved wonderfully accommodating to visitors. It is a good idea, however, to phone in advance. The day I played there he teamed me up with a local member, Tom McCorkindale, who basically sacrificed his own round in order to help me with mine. Such is the generosity of the Scottish golfing soul.

At Machrihanish, golf is still very much a classical linksland affair. The golf course is not "climate controlled"—

not subjected to scientific tinkering with water, drainage, and chemicals. Here you learn to appreciate the game as it has been played for many decades—in some cases, for many centuries. It is a humbling experience for the modernist in all of us to enjoy such elements in the raw.

CS

Scotland's Northern Links

Golf is entirely different along the sea. Winds play havoc with every airborne stroke. There are no trees to define the corridors of play. Crumpled fairways, surrounded by strange and wild plant life, appear worlds away from the crisp green lawns familiar to modern players. A golfer has not truly experienced the game without a journey over classic linksland.

Nothing surpasses Scotland's northern coast when it comes to seaside golf. Here along the North Sea, 100 miles above Glasgow or Edinburgh, at a latitude closer to the Arctic Circle than to Paris, the game's primitive beauty is on full display. These layouts may be too remote ever to host a British Open, but for generations now they have brought joy to the traveling golfer.

References to golf on the links at Dornoch date back to the seventeenth century. Today, Royal Dornoch Golf Club is widely ranked among the top-10 courses in the world. Located 40 miles above Inverness past Loch Ness, on an estuary that empties into the North Sea, these remote links feature a stunning array of holes.

The current course began to take shape in 1877 when Old Tom Morris, of St. Andrews and British Open fame, laid out 18 holes. A local lad named Donald Ross served his greenkeeping apprenticeship at Dornoch. After a year at St. Andrews and another season at Carnoustie, he returned here before establishing himself in the United States as a preeminent golf course architect. Visitors today to Royal Dornoch will no doubt spot similarities between its artistically shaped plateau greens and the putting surfaces which Ross himself later fashioned, say, at Pinehurst.

During the Second World War, the Royal Air Force requisitioned Dornoch for part of an airfield. The golf course was reclaimed from near-oblivion in 1946. The addition of a handful of new holes at the far end of the layout gave Dornoch its current configuration of eight holes out on the landward side and ten holes back, most of them along the sea to the left.

It's possible literally to tumble out of a guest room at the Royal Golf Hotel and find oneself on Dornoch's first tee. Don't be disarmed by the simplicity of this opening hole. The real drama starts at the third, where from a tee built into sandy headlands nearly the whole of the course sparkles before one's eyes. Purplish heather and yellow gorse plants surround this magical playing field, while off to the right, just beyond the line of primary dunes, the waves wash up on the beach. There are few scenes so perfectly framed as this first glimpse of Dornoch links.

The golf is superb, in large measure because the firm sandy turf will accommodate a wide range of shot-making. As with any seaside course, yardages are all but meaningless. The bent grass and native fescues prove receptive to bump and run shots. Players accustomed to dart-like target golf will simply have to make adjustments.

The slightest off-line shot on the par-three sixth hole will lead to a version of Ping-Pong between impossibly severe bunkers on one side of the green and a steep falloff on the other. Over at the bunkerless 14th, a maddening double dogleg par-four named "Foxy," the challenge resides in a succession of natural hollows and in a perched green that emerges from behind a dune.

There's no stuffiness at Dornoch, no pretense of exclusivity. All visitors are made to feel welcome in the clubhouse, and it is a simple matter to secure tee times in advance by writing. Besides the championship golf course, by the way, Dornoch also offers a very good second course called the Struie. Nor is there any shortage of daylight so far north; around the middle of June at Dornoch it is possible to golf from 4 a.m. to nearly midnight.

The area used to be extremely remote, but the opening of a bridge across the Dornoch Firth has made the trip considerably shorter. Indeed, for those long familiar with Royal Dornoch, it is hard not to regret the inevitable rise in traffic and trade that has resulted from the easier access.

In any case, there is now a second reason to make the long trek north: Carnegie Links at Skibo Castle. Carnegie Links is part of a 7,500 acre estate that used to belong to steel magnate Andrew Carnegie. He had left the country penniless, but returned as one of the world's richest men. In 1898, he commissioned a rather basic nine-hole golf course for himself and his closest friends. He died in 1919, and the golf course went to farmland during World War II. Meanwhile, the entire estate— with its magnificent castle, guest houses, fishing grounds, riding stable, and swimming pavilion—remained within the Carnegie family. In 1990, London business visionary and yachting enthusiast Peter de Savary came along with ambitious plans for Skibo as an all-encompassing retreat. Among those he hired to rebuild each component of the grounds was golf course architect Donald Steel.

A championship amateur golfer as well as fine golf journalist for many years, Steel has long been a proponent of using intelligence rather than armies of bulldozers in building worthy courses. At Skibo, there was no need to move heaven and earth. The land itself flowed so naturally that it was largely a matter of placing holes and then finding a routing that would tie them in. The result is a par-71 layout, with five sets of tees ranging from 5,436 yards to 6,671 from the very back. As with all links courses, however, distances account for next to nothing amid the winds and the constantly changing weather conditions. Sixteen of the holes are laid out in a broad east-west axis, and when the wind comes up, as it invariably does, you are either very much downwind or playing into its teeth.

The real beauty of golf at Skibo is that the features are all low-lying. The sandy soil enables the bunkers to be dug down deep rather than flashed up. The bunkers thereby function as whirlpools, with the effective area of a hazard about five times larger than its sand. Water there is, but none of it artificial. A number of holes play along the firth, the River Evelix, Loch Evelix, or intertidal salt marsh. And the care taken during construction to preserve the environment is evident in several areas native to a rare moss called "lichen heath."

Even modest elevation changes have a dramatic effect on linksland. A green built up on a dune ridge at the 152-yard par-three third hole makes it imperative that you get the ball up, while the 267-yard par-four 17th hole plays just downhill enough so that you are tempted to go for the green off the tee. Of course, to do so, you have to work the prevailing left to right crosswind by starting the ball out over Dornoch Firth. If the tee shot comes down just a bit short there are enough deep, revetted bunkers to make you wish you had laid up well short.

Golf at Skibo is usually part of a comprehensive guest plan. A single price of 450 pounds sterling ($720), double occupancy, covers anything and everything you could imagine without question—overwhelming meals served at an oak dining table that seats 24; use of the trap and skeet club; private fishing instruction; and overnight accommodations in museum-piece quality Edwardian guest salons. We are, after all, talking about a tenth century castle, with a snooker parlor that looks like Andrew Carnegie just stepped out and a dramatic lobby, replete with overhead walkway and a double stairway, that could handle the cast *and* audience of "Phantom of the Opera." Drives through the countryside can even be arranged in one of Skibo's Rolls Royces.

Don't panic at the price. You can either afford it or you can't, and if you can, you don't worry. If you can't, you stay down the road in Dornoch and pay a daily green fee of 50 pounds ($80).

Another taste of seaside golf can be found a short drive east of Culloden in the town of Nairn. Founded in 1887, Nairn Golf Club owes its character to the design work of five-time British Open champion James Braid, among whose other Scottish credits are the Kings and Queens Courses at Gleneagles and Dalmahoy East, site of the 1990 Solheim Cup. Braid's reliance upon sunken, sod-walled bunkers at Nairn gives this 6,722 yard, par-72 course its distinctive look.

The opening holes run due west along the Moray Coast. At the eighth tee, the course turns back inland across dramatically sloping ground. The loveliest vista comes at the downhill par-four 15th, which from a well-elevated tee set back in the woods looks north out to sea.

The beach in front of the golf course provides the perfect setting for an evening stroll. Just a few hundred yards behind the clubhouse sits the Golf View Hotel, with its creaky turn-of-the-century comforts. Nairn, by the way, is the first of a dozen or more courses strung along the southern shore of the Moray Firth. This stretch of coastline deserves more attention from golf travelers because a succession of fishing villages, including Lossiemouth, Buckie, Macduff, and Fraserburgh, all have worthy seaside links.

Without doubt the most distinctive of these can be found at Cullen, 50 miles east of Nairn, halfway to Peterhead. Cullen Golf Club originated in 1879. Only 4,610 yards short, this par-63 course recalls a distant era of gutta-percha golf balls and hickory shaft clubs. The greens, little more than modest ovals, have virtually no character. The bunkering is nothing less than antiquated, and on a handful of holes the green cannot be seen from the approach area.

What makes Cullen memorable is its setting—squeezed into a narrow front of beach and craggy headline. The holes weave their way in and around tall columns of exposed rock called sea-stacks. Over thousands of years, the waters crashing in off the sea nibbled away at the coastline. These stone towers, some 80 to 100 feet tall, miraculously survived nature's savagery.

The course starts and ends on low-lying dunesland, but at the second hole, the golfer ascends a steep slope to a headland where the next five holes teeter on the brink. Then comes as breathtaking a hole as can be found in all of golf. The tee at the par-three, 231-yard seventh is a launching pad perched on a jagged sea-stack. The drive here seems to float forever before coming back to earth.

Leave the wildest golf course for last lest anything afterward suffer by comparison. Cruden Bay Golf Club offers unrelenting linksland. Located in the northeast corner of the Buchan Peninsula, hard by the North Sea between the port cities of Peterhead and Aberdeen, Cruden Bay has quietly yet deservedly become recognized by knowledgeable golf travelers for the power of its seaside presence.

The course at Cruden Bay sprang into life a century ago as the focal point of an ambitious undertaking by the Great North of Scotland Railway Company. As a resort complex the project failed, but in large measure due to the talents of course designers Tom Simpson and Herbert Fowler in 1926, the course became a showpiece of natural feature work.

The secret of Cruden Bay's genius lies in its routing. The holes, laid out on a stretch of dunesland between town and the beach, describe the figure of an hour-glass. The third hole, a par-four of only 286 yards, pitches and rolls like the sea itself and culminates with a green so steeply banked that its surface seems in eternal motion. The eighth hole, another par-four of minuscule length, is nestled into a natural amphitheater that could surely hold 20,000 spectators. And the 14th green, sunken into a hollow and blind behind a raised bunker, looks more like an oversized bathtub than a putting surface.

Fairways that undulate through massive dunes; greens seemingly hanging on a ledge for dear life; bunkers placed just where a perfect shot would land; let all who tread this sacred ground abandon modern expectations of manicured turf and tree-lined fairways. There is nothing to compare to the look and feel of these wild turfs—marram grass, fescues, and heathery roughs, and all the while the ferocious sound and sight of the sea pounding away. As if more mystery were needed, the ruins of Slains Castle, the inspiration for Bram Stoker's "Dracula," preside just to the north of Cruden Bay and are easily visible on the opening and closing holes.

Golf at Cruden Bay is enjoying something of a boom these days, in large part thanks to oil money. The North Sea pipeline, after all, touches land just south of the 12th green. Today there are ambitious plans for a new clubhouse. Let's only hope that the antiquated charm of the course does not get lost in the process. A good place to start might be in rehabilitating the old abandoned professional's shed behind the first tee. The quaint green wooden building served Cruden Bay for decades, but now sits sadly empty. A sign of the times, and a reminder as well, of the beauty of Scottish linksland.

∞

Western Ireland: The Wind, the Sea and the Guinness

The golfing traveler who comes to the west coast of Ireland has chosen very wisely, for not far from Ireland's international airport at Shannon lie three distinct and memorable courses: Ballybunion, Lahinch, and Connemara. Each venue runs through wild dunes that overlook the Atlantic Ocean. And each course is tendered by the friendliest people in all of golf. The weather will likely be raw, but the clubhouse is always warm. And if the wind and the sea don't sweep you off your feet, the beer surely will.

Our week-long trip left my wife and me little time to squander. Minutes after arriving at the airport we were off on our golfing venture—around the Shannon Estuary to Ballybunion, 70 miles away in County Kerry.

Two hours later we arrived at The Marine Hotel, only a short walk along a main road from the golf course. The remains of a medieval fortress rose up on the cliffs just in front of the hotel, and down below, nestled in a cove, was a protected beach about a mile long. The hotel was small, with only 10 guest rooms, but the rates were modest and all was comfortable. Most endearing was the "golfy" atmosphere of the lobby/bar. Scenes of famous courses adorned the walls, and almost all the guests we met were there to play Ballybunion.

As we arrived at the clubhouse we found French, German, Swedish, and American players in the parking lot preparing to play. All had come to play Ballybunion's Old Course. To reduce the burdens upon the layout, the management in the mid-1980s had hired the distinguished golf architect, Robert Trent Jones, Sr., to build another course on dunes adjacent to the old layout. The New Course, however, is best thought of as a warm-up for the real thing. The holes just don't work because they are forced upon the land. It has proved nearly impossible to get visitors to play the thing, with the result being much money squandered by the club and a good site gone to waste.

The Old Course is another matter. First built in 1906, it is quite simply one of the most dramatic, yet also the fairest, of all links courses in the world. The first five holes are reasonably flat, and though sound, not especially memorable. But things start getting interesting at the 361-yard sixth, where a narrow little fairway leads to an unbunkered green that is easy to hit and terribly difficult to hold.

At the seventh tee, the Old Course reveals itself as a stunning example of natural seaside golf. The long four-par seventh runs atop the beach to a green sited so precariously close to the sea that several years ago parts of the putting surface collapsed into the Atlantic Ocean. An expensive plan designed to fight the erosion of sand has literally saved the hole—and the golf course—from disaster. Successive holes move up and down and through rolling sand hills, at times tantalizingly close to the sea. The par-four 10th, only 358 yards, calls for a second shot which, if hit just a tad leftward, will sail easily onto the beach below and out of play. The 15th hole, a very long, picturesque three-par, features a green partially hidden by dunes. Between the tee and the landing area there's nothing but broken ground, and the shot, depending upon the wind, can be anything from a mid-iron to a driver and a prayer.

We finished this hole and hoped for relief but found none. Sixteen was a dramatically narrow, slightly uphill five-par of 486 yards. The second shot here has to negotiate a defile that cuts through two massive sand dunes. The four of us, two players and two caddies, had nearly to walk single file through the approach area. The 17th hole then tumbled us back down toward the sea, and 18, an uphill four-par, finally brought us back to the warmth of the clubhouse. Here, Ballybunion's Club

Secretary, Mr. Sean Walsh, plied us with the pride of Ireland: the dark, stout, frothy Guinness beer. Two pints, and we were ready for another go at the Old Course.

Then, on to Lahinch in County Clare. A ferry traverses the Shannon River between Tarbert and Killimer, and this enabled us to keep the drive down to about 60 miles. Lahinch gets less play than Ballybunion, and there had been no trouble arranging our rounds through the acting club secretary there, Mr. Con McGovern.

As for accommodations, well, the place to stay for golfers seems to be the Aberdeen Arms Hotel, a 32-room inn and restaurant run by the Vaughan family. Michael Vaughan, Sr. and his son, Michael, Jr. proved eminently knowledgeable about local history and they know how to accommodate golfers: early breakfasts, wonderful tales of golf at Lahinch, and a keen sense of what to do and see in County Clare. A real treat came when they arranged for us to have dinner with one of the true characters of Lahinch golf: Mr. Austin Slattery, "Brudd" to everyone who meets him, who for 30 years oversaw life at the club and who still visits the course most days.

The Old Course at Lahinch could host the Irish Open tomorrow. It calls for an unshakably sound game, leaving no room for stray drives, indecisive approaches, or weakly struck putts. The fairways amble through all manner of hillocks and mounds without ever leaving the golfer uncertain about proper lines of play. And what a pedigree. First designed by Old Tom Morris in 1893, then rebuilt by Alister MacKenzie in 1927, the course is both quaint and modern, quirky and rugged.

Take, for example, the sixth hole, the 156 yard, par-three "Dell" hole which plays into the prevailing wind. Three huge dunes seem to engulf the green. The flag, let alone the putting surface, was nowhere to be seen from the tee. My caddie, Michael O'Connor, handed me a three-iron, pointed to a white stone marker on the near hill, and urged me to fly the ball over it. Modern golfers may not like such blind shots, but who cares? The hole is a museum piece and deserves a place in the golfing world. Then there's the 12th hole, a long, severe par-four over a fairway cantered from right to left that runs tight along the banks of the Inagh River.

And of course the goats: a trio of them, collectively relied upon, as local lore has it, to foretell the weather. At night they hang out by the clubhouse, by day they'll wander out onto the links. Unless rain or storms are in the air, in which case they find their way back to take cover near the pro shop.

Around Lahinch there's lots to do: sightseeing at the Cliffs of Moher with their 300-foot sheer fall into the Atlantic. There's also the best folk music in all of Ireland at McGann's in nearby Doolin. And about 20 miles north in Ballyvaughan is an exceedingly good restaurant called Clare's.

A three-hour drive north of Lahinch around Galway Bay brought us into County Galway and the village of Clifden. This is the cultural center of Western Ireland as well as a regional fishing capital.

The Connemara Golf Club is actually located 10 miles below Clifden in Ballyconneely. It is a recent venture, built only in 1973 by an association of local businessmen who hired architect Eddie Hackett. On the day we arrived there the restaurant/bar at the course was overflowing with local golfers and their families. It was a comfortable atmosphere, nothing stuffy about it. Foreign visitors are just discovering Connemara and are warmly welcomed at the club. Outside, a 50-mph wind raged, and after warming ourselves up with Irish coffee we went out to see if golf was at all possible.

The beautiful thing about well-built seaside courses is that they hold up under all kinds of weather. Connemara was no exception. The fairways are wide, and though the approaches are much narrower, there were just enough openings to the greens for us to run the ball up rather than try to carry it on. The front nine was not entirely memorable, but at the eighth tee the course began to utilize the natural swales and flow of dunes. This proved a killer of a four-par, 459 yards into the force-nine gale. Patience was required here, for there was little else to do but swing easily, keep the ball in play, and try, vainly as it turned out, to reach the green in three.

The back nine was a wondrously routed set of holes that glided up and down through exposed limestone and deep sands. The par-three 13th, 207 yards, starts from a tee placed amid exposed rock and then runs across a tiny field to a delicately bunkered green. At the 18th tee we found ourselves looking from on high to a wide fairway below, the hills of County Galway to the left, and over on the right the waters of the Atlantic crashing onto the rocks. Happily, this last hole, a five-par, played downwind and was reachable with two bold shots skirting the out-of-bounds right. When we traipsed off the green, exhausted from battling the wind, the men's golf captain, Mr. John P. Roche, welcomed us over to the bar for— what else?—yet another pint of Guinness.

That night we warmed ourselves at the Abbeyglen Castle, a 40-room hotel that sits atop a canyon overlooking Clifden harbor. With another fine dinner behind us, we went out for a walk down to the town. Early the next morning we would have to return to Shannon Airport for the flight home to the States. It had only been a week on Ireland's west coast, and as we walked through the pastel and blue store fronts of downtown Clifden we began to reminisce about the trip, as if the golf and the sights were already behind us. And of course in a way they were. But we felt lucky at having come to know such beautiful courses—powerful reminders of what golf everywhere in the world can be.

8

Treasure Hunting

Astoria: A Coastal Oregon Gem

There's nothing more exciting in golf architecture than stumbling upon an unknown course that proves to be a stunner. The much-abused term for this is, of course, "a hidden gem." In a media-saturated age like ours, with jet-set travel now commonplace, it's hard to imagine something as large as a golf course evading detection. More likely, it's a matter of a solid golf course remaining locally well-regarded but without a national reputation.

Such is the case out in coastal Oregon with the Astoria Golf and Country Club. The course sits near the seaside town of Warrenton, 85 miles northwest of Portland. The Pacific Ocean is but one mile from the first tee, and though there is no sound or sight of its waters, the winds do come raging in. More important is the linksland soil, for Astoria is built upon a pure base of sand. Rows of sand dunes, to be precise, many of them 40 feet high, that run on a north-south axis. Fourteen of Astoria's holes are routed parallel to them. The result is unlike anything to be experienced in this hemisphere.

Astoria G&CC dates back to 1923, when a group of gentlemen, most of them from the nearby fishing port of Astoria, decided to build a private club. A Mr. R.C. Jack Asbury, who was a wealthy amateur golfer and who was also purported to be an architect and engineer, was asked to lay out and build the course in exchange for a lifetime membership. His plan called for the holes to be routed in an east-west fashion, with play proceeding perpendicular to (that is, up, over, and across) the distinctive dunes lines.

The membership had the good sense to dismiss these plans and instead turned to their president, Mr. Charles Halderman, and to George Junor, who would become the club's first greenkeeper. The course they built, intact today with very minor variation, is among the great unknown secrets of American course architecture.

The par-72 layout stretches to 6,494 yards, with a slope of 120 and a 71.0 rating. But as with all distinctive courses, such numbers tell nothing of the real tale. The holes snuggle perfectly in place, each ensconced in its own native dwelling, surrounded by dunes, framed by native beach grasses, and breathtakingly simple in conception.

Only two of the par-fours so much as dogleg, and then only slightly. The three par-fives come bunched up within a stretch of four holes in the middle of the course. Most of the greens are little more than oval-shaped. But then, who needs complexity, or to conform to mechanical rules of balance and design when the piece of ground you're working with looks as crumpled and corduroy-like as this?

Since before World War II, the club has been known as "the St. Andrews of the Pacific." This was never meant to be an accurate description, and in any case, there is not even a fleeting resemblance. But in those days, Astoria's fairways were lined with vast thickets of Scotch broom. Finally, when a few pennies started accumulating in the club's meager treasury, officials removed this growth. In 1951 they planted irregular stands and rows of coastal pines to delineate corridors of play.

The ocean breezes have given these trees an appropriately weather-beaten look. The rough grass is now some version of native beach grass, which looks and plays like a combination of rye gone to seed and wild fine fescues. In any case, the juxtaposition of textures and colors gives Astoria a classical look that is all too rare today. At the same time, superintendent Bill Winslow has cultivated a vibrant carpet of *Poa annua* and rye on the tees, greens, and fairways.

The opening hole is set alongside a sprawling dune, but this is nothing compared to what awaits at the third. Here on a 378-yard par-four, the fairway, I swear, is only 12 yards wide and sits like the bottom of a U-shaped groove between two enormous parallel dunes that run in straight lines from tee to green. Talk about containment mounding! The effect is overwhelming. And then the chase is on.

There are so many amazing holes here. The fifth is a demanding Cape hole across a lake to a steeply (in fact, too steeply) banked green. The ninth is a par-five calling for a drive across a watercourse to a fairway that cants from right to left. The 129-yard par-three 10th hole, by contrast, is little more than an extension of the clubhouse patio and runs dead along the height of a dune.

Like many classical courses, this one has also had its wooden clubhouse burn down, though not until 1968. And while a purist might rant and rave about the tree plantings, in fact they work to give some definition without intruding upon play, unless you hook or slice the ball like crazy into a parallel fairway.

With the weather amenable for golf year-round, Astoria logs about 47,000 rounds annually. Somehow, the tees and greens hold up despite being undersized for the traffic. The course currently has an antiquated irrigation system of quick couplers. In order to maintain turf, water has to be applied wholesale, with the result being fairway and greenside areas that are less amenable to the bump and run game than they should be. But that will soon be solved with installation of an automated system that will enable Astoria to water more selectively without drenching the whole course.

A few minor changes in the layout have been made over the years. The second green was moved forward to avoid a blind approach to a congested area. The 10th tee was repositioned slightly. But that's all, and that's as it should be. The last thing Astoria needs is to lengthen itself, build new holes, or make itself a modern tournament venue. Architects looking for revision work need not apply.

Courses like Astoria (and I'm not sure there are any) are living museum pieces demonstrating the art of natural design. With all the hype about top-100 lists and best new this and that, the real poverty of the ratings game is that an Astoria G&CC doesn't stand a chance. Too short; not resistant to scoring; and it lacks in what they like to call design-balance. Hogwash.

Besides, it's better to stay out of the spotlight. That leaves the course for the membership, and they know they have something special. Indeed, half of Astoria's members come from the upscale Portland golf clubs. They have second homes along the coast and use Astoria as a getaway club. There are also many local truck drivers, school teachers, and wage earners who cherish Astoria as their primary golf club. With a course like this, there's no need for them to go anywhere else.

◌

The Orchards: Superintendent Revives Rundown Ross Treasure

Paul Jamrog, golf course superintendent at The Orchards, in South Hadley, Massachusetts, was looking for old photographs.

"We've come a long way in making this course look the way Donald Ross probably intended it," said Jamrog when I spoke with him in July 1988, "but we'd still like to see what the old bunkers and greens actually looked like."

Ross came upon this 200-acre site back in 1922 at the behest of local textile magnate Joseph Skinner. His daughter, Elisabeth Skinner, had taken to golf but lacked a regular outlet. So Dad presented her with a nine-hole course. Five years later, Ross returned to revise the layout and to add another nine. Except for the rebuilding of two greens in the late-1970s, the golf course has remained untouched ever since. Architecture aficionados call it "pure Ross."

The United States Golf Association was so taken by this previously unheralded layout that in 1987 it held the National Girls' Junior Amateur there. Frank Hannigan, then the USGA Senior Executive Director, could barely contain his joy over his discovery. "I can't wait to tell Ben Crenshaw about this course," he said as he walked down the fourth fairway.

Longtime host professional Bob Bontempo has legitimate

hopes that the course might host a U.S. Women's Amateur some day. Indeed, the late 1980s were heady days at The Orchards. But things weren't always that way. When Jamrog first arrived here in 1984 at the base of the Holyoke Range in west central Massachusetts, the course was unkempt.

Poa annua and crabgrass had infested the course. The putting surfaces all appeared rounded off. Many of the bunker faces were in disrepair and the traps had been so carelessly raked that the sand overspilled them to the point where the bunkers lacked clear definition or shape.

The course drained so poorly that at times it looked like a bog. And the natural contours of the rolling land were scarcely visible to the golfer because all the fairways were being mowed in a straight line from tee to green. The condition of the course scarcely befitted its pedigree.

The Skinner family had looked after the course until 1941, when it sold The Orchards to an adjacent school, Mount Holyoke College. John Bratula, a member since 1946, recalls that "the fairways and greens were mowed once a week by the College staff—with the same lawn mower used for the campus grounds. At the same height setting. As for the rough, well, they never really cut it. Though about twice a year the local farmers would come and haul the clippings off for hay."

Maintenance became somewhat more sophisticated in the 1950s, what with the introduction of a manually operated watering system and the use of gang mowers. But Jamrog claims that the introduction of these modern conveniences simply brought new problems to The Orchards.

"The college maintenance crew was unionized, and therefore costly. In order to save labor costs they minimized the hand cutting. Greens were cut with triplex riding mowers, and this led to a rounding off of the original putting surfaces. Mechanized bunker rakes—the ones you ride—enabled one worker to attend to all the sand hazards, but at the cost of gradually if imperceptively enlarging the bunkers each time they were worked over. And instead of hand-cutting the mounds and bunker faces, they used motorized mowers, and this took its toll on surface soil and the root system. It led to a lot of erosion."

Jamrog figured that his first task was to get some good grasses back onto the course. He began with a massive seeding of ryes, a grass that, if not ideal, would at least take quickly.

Once the ryes had spread he then began the full conversion over to bent grass fairways. These provide the best playing turf, and when they take root, their stolons serve to regenerate ever more grass. On greens and tees Jamrog followed the re-seeding program with heavy doses of a fertilizer compound called Tupersan. Siduron, a chemical in the Tupersan, literally holds down the crabgrass while enabling the bent grass stolons to come through.

As part of the new regimen, Jamrog brought back hand-mowing for the greens and tees in order to control their shaping. Over the years, they had been winnowed down, and Jamrog spent a lot of time figuring out how the original playing areas were supposed to look. Eventually, greens were brought out to include mounds and rolls which had earlier become neglected as the putting surfaces shrank.

To accomplish all this, the maintenance staff had to be expanded. Back in 1984, Jamrog was the only full-time, year-round member of the greens staff. Four years later he was one of four, and he enjoyed the help of six others in-season. As Jamrog says, "that's the price for having a golf course in first-rate shape."

Out on the course, Jamrog began several practices that not all members agreed with. He narrowed the fairways, contour-mowed them, and then allowed the wild-looking brownish fescues to grow back unkempt. Fairways 50-yards wide might have been welcome to some of the golfers, but such widths left the holes looking nondescript, void of definition. Narrowing the fairways enabled Jamrog to move the lines of play by mowing in a more sweeping fashion. And finally, Jamrog abandoned altogether the practice of cutting down the rough. The plan was simply to bring back the fescues out there.

Jamrog explained this at length. "What had been seeded into the golf course when Donald Ross designed and built it was mainly fescues, and they were everywhere. At that time they didn't have the variety of grasses that we have available now. Really, the look of the golf course should be to let those fescues grow up and then to let them go dormant in the summer months. That's the type of look, the Scottish look, that had been intended for the golf course. It had been mowed down in previous years and now we're trying to revive those areas. More and more we try to sneak it in before some of the members have a chance to protest. And you can't blame them, because that's what they were used to and because the course plays somewhat tougher with the fescues. But it just looks right. It looks the way it was designed. And really, you shouldn't try to change anything about the course."

But then a dilemma arose, because in order to restore the course, some changes would be necessary. The question is, which ones? What with all the soil erosion and the loss of shape in the greens, certain alterations would be called for, if the point were to restore the original look. But here, Jamrog proceeded cautiously.

A few years earlier, it turns out, two of the greens on the front side were completely rebuilt: dug out, resodded, recontoured, and rebunkered, all overseen by a regional designer named Al Zikorus. The outcome, unanimously attested to by membership, staff, and guests alike, was disastrous. As one member said, "the greens don't look right, they don't play right, and they just don't belong out there."

By all accounts, the two greens, at the third and eighth holes, were in serious disrepair and had required work. But the results proved so ungainly that the membership since became very edgy whenever anyone at The Orchards talked about reconstruction. Even if the procedure were purely restorative, the members basically wanted nothing to do with it.

Brian Silva, a Massachusetts-based architect, was brought in to consult with the greens committee on measures to revive the course. But modest as Silva's master plan was, the membership protested. The message was clear. Be careful before you operate on the patient, so to speak. Given the sensitivities of the membership, Jamrog worked very carefully with the green committee before undertaking any changes at all.

In his first few years, Jamrog restored The Orchards by a maintenance program alone, without any real reconstruction. But as Jamrog then saw it, the condition of the course had been sufficiently improved upon so that players could begin to see the virtues of its original design features.

The question became whether reconstruction was called for in order to bring out the course's historic character. The bunkers needed rebuilding, for instance, and the brook system that ran through the course, including the drainage ponds, also required attention. Furthermore, several bunkers that were "snuck in" over the years after Ross built The Orchards needed, in Jamrog's views, to be taken out.

This all became subject to serious discussion with the concerned membership, and as Jamrog saw it, this was to be welcomed, not regretted. For The Orchards began to thrive due to its vigorous new maintenance program. The membership and staff became understandably proud—and therefore protective—of what they had. So careful were they that a delegation of members went down to Pinehurst, North Carolina, and discovered, among Donald Ross' papers there, his original sketches for some of the holes at The Orchards.

There's a lesson in Jamrog's pioneering work. To be able to appreciate the design features of a classical golf course, the venue has to be brought to top-notch playing condition. That means the turf, the cut, and the shape of greens, tees, and fairways. Once the course is in good condition, you can begin searching for its classical features. And then you can haul out those old photographs to compare how the course looks, and to decide whether it ought to look more like the way its designer intended.

The Fine Art of Restoration

Martin Kantor is a prominent New York dentist, but the toughest teeth he's ever had to pull are those of his own membership at Engineers CC. As green chairman of a venerable Long Island club, he's shepherding an ambitious restoration plan designed to return the club to its glory years. A layout that hosted the 1919 PGA Championship and the 1921 U.S. Amateur, he figures, is a layout that deserves to be taken seriously three-quarters of a century later.

His efforts are not alone. Throughout the United States, clubs are taking a serious look at their architectural heritage. A generation ago, the buzzwords were "renovation" and "modernization." Today, the trend is toward classical restoration. It's part of an effort to preserve traditional values. Decisive in this is a generation of younger architects whose primary concern is less to impose their signature on a course than to bring out its native subtlety and charm.

Ron Prichard styles himself a purist when it comes to preservation. He's designed his share of new courses, including the TPC at Southwinds near Memphis. But his real loves are the traditional layouts. His portfolio today includes Metacomet Country Club, a 1921 Donald Ross gem outside Providence, Rhode Island, as well as several courses designed by such Ross contemporaries as Alex Findlay, Willie Park, Jr., and Robert White. For Prichard, the allure of classical courses is that their creators knew how to utilize good land. "These people had a very special perception of the game," says Prichard, "and they were much more generous than architects today in establishing playing areas. There was only one set of tees, and par was really meaningless. There was never a full shot penalty, and they created intricate greens. They worked with a certain sense of freedom and were not out to embarrass or humiliate players."

In the 1950s and '60s, it was standard for architects to renovate older courses by lengthening holes and fortifying greens. The paradigm case for this modernization was Robert Trent Jones' recasting of Donald Ross' Oakland Hills CC outside Detroit for the 1951 U.S. Open. Jones undertook a similar, if somewhat less grandiose, project for Baltusrol prior to the 1954 U.S. Open. The pattern was set, though it was not always executed with care, and in many cases, Jones himself obliterated original features, all in the name of defending par off the tee. Nowhere was the impact more devastating than at Aronimink, near Philadelphia, where in 1989 he and his design associate Roger Rulewich carelessly pinched every landing area with punitive bunkers. Luckily, they left intact the original routing and the putting grounds. Once again, Ron Prichard has been called in to the rescue.

With too many designers, heavy-handed surgery became standard operating procedure—not only for clubs hosting national championships, but also for private country clubs and municipal layouts seeking to stay competitive. All too often clubs tried to improve upon what they perceived as their weakest holes. But in many cases, these were precisely the short and interesting ones, often the only holes members could reach in regulation.

There was a price paid along the way. A certain charm in the ground game and in the native flow of landforms was threatened. It may well have been appropriate to adapt some older 6,400-yard courses to the high-tech, high-power demands of modern tournament play. But a number of observers say that the shortcomings of such reconstruction were reached in the work done by George and Tom Fazio at Inverness prior to the 1979 U.S. Open and at Oak Hill for the 1980 PGA. Quite simply, their work was clumsy and grossly out of character with established features. Traditionalists groaned.

To be sure, there have been good reasons for tinkering. For one thing, courses are themselves organic artifacts, subject to natural erosion and siltation. Add to that the wear and tear normally associated with golf traffic and there's no wonder that courses begin to look ragged. The lips of bunkers build up from sand; *Poa annua* turf infests bent grass, and trees extend their canopies to close down established corridors of play.

Changes in maintenance techniques also take their toll. Tillinghast himself went around the country in the 1930s removing dozens of bunkers from his and other architects' courses, all in the name of saving money for clubs strapped with extensive labor costs. By the 1960s, superintendents were ride-mowing their greens rather than hand-walking them with smaller mowers. The result, usually, was that intricately shaped putting surfaces became rounded off and reduced in size to little more than nondescript circles. The advent of motorized trap rakes was the death knell for those small, elaborate bunkers that had been the trademark of classical stylists. Irrigation systems and the introduction of heavily watered bent grass fairways also rendered obsolete the firm, wide-open style of older, ryegrass playing surfaces.

Matters were made worse by the proclivity of green committees to plant ornamental trees—indeed, to engage in wholesale plantings as a way of imposing a parkland atmosphere. Courses like Oakmont (1903), San Francisco GC (1915), and Winged Foot (1923) were windswept and devoid of trees when they opened. Gradually, they became home to thousands of trees, and their playing characteristics were altered fundamentally. A game meant to be played on the ground now had to be played in the air.

Is it possible to go back to what was originally there? Architects will tell you it depends on what was there in the first place, and whether the club really wants to return. Does restoration on a Ross course mean bringing back the cross bunkers 120 yards off the tees? Cutting down all the trees? How about removing the irrigation system and eliminating the forward tees?

When Ben Crenshaw and his design associate Bill Coore were hired to restore Tillinghast's Brook Hollow in Dallas, they found aerial photos from the 1930s that showed no trees and hundreds of bunkers. The course they looked at in the 1990s had thousands of trees and perhaps only one-third as many bunkers. A pure restoration was out of the question, as the membership was long familiar with a different course than was "originally" there. The result was a reconstruction, not a pure restoration, that cleansed the soil of sediments, eliminated some 225 trees, and recast the bunkers lightly so as to make them look more natural.

All restoration is site-specific. It depends upon what's there and the integrity of the design. Much of what passes for restoration is in fact an interpretation on the architect's part regarding what the designer initially had in mind or what that designer might build today. Strategic bunkers 140 yards off the tee may need to be moved back to 190 yards, for instance. And steep putting surfaces that were functional in one era may be out-of-date in an era characterized by slick speeds and the Stimpmeter.

Sometimes, pure restoration is possible. At National Golf Links in Southampton, Long Island, course superintendent Karl Olson has been working for a decade with archeological precision in restoring to full size the greens and playing areas of Charles Blair Macdonald's gothic masterpiece. Tree and shrub growth has been cleared away to reveal long-lost bunkers and sand mounds 30 yards off the edge of playing areas. The original putting surfaces averaged about 14,000 square feet. Olson has been nursing them back from roughly half that size and plans to bring them up to 10,000 square feet.

The toughest aspect of course renovation is not the dirt work but the in-house politics. Clubs that are torn by factions and competing agendas are notoriously difficult to work with. The ideal situation, says Crenshaw, is "a club that's proud of its course, that has accurate archives, and where the people in charge are in concert with each other."

When it comes to accurate information, a key figure in restoration projects has been Florida-based golf course renovator Ed Connor. He has created a means of laser-measuring existing contours so that greens can be reconstructed and duplicated. The technique enabled designers to redo the greens at such marquee courses as Pinehurst #2 and Pebble Beach (as well as at Riviera, but with less success). Connor cautions that pure restoration is not always in order. "Lasering enables preservation—where there is something to preserve. It all depends upon what's there."

Course architect Brian Silva says that "I just don't know that pure restoration is applicable to 10,000 courses—but it might be for 200." In such work, controversy abounds, especially for someone who "claims" to understand Ross so well. Just ask Silva himself. He has worked at several high-profile courses, including Five Farms outside Baltimore and such Ross layouts as Interlachen in Minneapolis, Orlando CC, and Sara Bay in Sarasota, Florida. Up in Connecticut, however, he inadvertently contributed to the creation of the Donald Ross Society when a group of members at the Ross-designed Wampanoag Country Club in West Hartford were appalled at Silva's awkward redesign work there.

Today, the Donald Ross Society claims 1,350 members nationwide, including a dozen practicing course architects. It has worked with a North Carolinian named W. Pete Jones to mine the Ross archives in Pinehurst and exhaustively document the fate of the 413 known Ross courses. Where possible, the Society now makes records available to clubs interested in course restoration.

There is always the fear that such enthusiasm can reach the level of dogma. Was every Ross feature brilliant? Can a debate today about placement of bunkers be settled by referring to Ross' plans?

Nevertheless, a trend is observable these days whereby older courses are first asking themselves about the value of what they have before they go about changing it. For the 1994 U.S. Open, Oakmont had architect Arthur Hills help bring the course back somewhat to its older, wider-playing character, in part by removing some 200 hardwoods. A more extensive project has been underway at San Francisco GC, which many consider to be Tillinghast's finest sculpture. Working in-house, the club has removed some 500 trees. The membership is now enjoying vistas it didn't even know existed.

Perhaps all those lists of "100 best" courses have had an effect on the public's awareness of fine design. Perceptions have also been fine-tuned by the USGA's success in hosting the 1986 U.S. Open at Shinnecock Hills, an old-fashioned, links-style venue to which the Open returned in 1995. The cause of classical restoration, as distinct from modern renovation, was surely aided by Rees Jones' sensitive preparation work at The Country Club in Brookline, Massachusetts for the 1988 U.S. Open.

Moreover, anyone interested in restoration can now consult a single book, Geoffrey Cornish and Ron Whitten's *The Architects of Golf* (previously, *The Golf Course*) for reliable data on who designed what and when.

Nothing poses a greater threat to classical courses than the distances the golf ball can now travel. Prichard is not alone in singling out the game's governing body on this. "Because the USGA," he says, "hasn't had enough courage to review its criteria on equipment, and perhaps to turn a few pages back, most of our brilliant classical courses are becoming museum pieces for championship play."

A number of gifted architects are now establishing themselves as connoisseurs, and saviors, of classical design. Moreover, they are willing to devote long hours tracking down archives and interviewing senior members in order to get a clearer sense of what the course used to look like and what the designer intended. It is also mandatory that long hours be spent on-site accompanying the shaper, massaging each roll and twist of earth. In most cases, the spade work of restoration is not as lucrative as new course assignments. But it is nonetheless important as a way of preserving the game's traditions.

While many established architects shy away from the work, some younger designers are actively making a name for themselves in the field. Stephen Kay's work at Winchester CC in Massachusetts is exemplary for its sensitive approach to rebuilding a Ross layout. Ron Forse has garnered similar acclaim for his restoration at Hyannisport GC, an old Donald Ross-Alex Findlay layout. On Long Island, Tom Doak and design associate/shaper Gil Hanse highlighted a number of long-obscured Macdonald features at The Creek Club, including a reverse Redan hole. At Garden City GC, Doak says, "The basic task was to correct the construction and design mistakes that had been made in the 1960s." He squared off the low-profile tees, rebuilt quirky old traps in place, and added fairway bunkers to a Walter Travis-Devereux Emmet masterpiece that complemented the established hazards.

Hanse now has his own projects, including Engineers CC. There he (and dentist/green chairman Martin Kantor) hope to bring back to full size the wildly undulating putting surfaces that Herbert Strong had first built. Plans also call for extensive tree pruning and removal, cultivation of native grasses in the rough, and perhaps even a revival of the famed old "2 or 20" hole, the 103-yard par-three 14th that was named after the wide range of scores readily possible there.

In a widely publicized exhibition at Engineers in 1920, both Bobby Jones and Gene Sarazen recorded double figures on the hole. It has since been taken out of rotation, effectively pushed aside by a modern par-three hole, 218 yards to the dullest green on the course. There is no better example of why restoration is needed. With a little finagling of the routing, the "2 or 20" can be brought back. A hole devilish enough for Jones and Sarazen is a hole good enough for the ages.

9

Classical
Tracks

Pine Valley

Playing Pine Valley in New Jersey is like being transported to some otherworldly game preserve, where the golfer is confronted by one armored monster after another. Sometimes the golfing prince will slay the dragon. Sometimes he will escape the poisonous snakes. But let him breathe a momentary sigh and all of a sudden a hawk will swoop by and pluck away his crown.

The temptation is strong to side with those who claim Pine Valley as the world's greatest golf course. At the very entrance to this club you get the sense that something is different about the place. The course occupies a separate borough, replete with its own mayor.

Located about 18 miles southeast of Philadelphia, in the sandy pine barrens of lower New Jersey, Pine Valley has held center stage in the history of golf course architecture for three-quarters of a century. The course was the brainchild of Philadelphia hotelier George Crump. He was part of a distinguished group of local golfers searching for ground upon which to build a course playable year-round. Crump chose a lot that, according to contemporary press reports, was frighteningly unsuited for course development.

Crump had made a whirlwind golf tour of Britain. He was determined to capture some of the look and feel of the parkland English courses. To this end, he drew upon the advice of British architect H.S. Colt. Crump had been particularly impressed by Colt's design of Sunningdale, outside London.

Black and white photographs of the construction process hang today in the Pine Valley clubhouse. Some of them have also been reprinted in Mr. Warner Shelly's excellently researched history of Pine Valley Golf Club. The photos depict strangely primitive land undergoing transformation through painstaking labor. The scenes are reminiscent of what Soviet agriculture looked like after the Russian Revolution.

A wood-burning steam winch uprooted over 22,000 trees, many of which were cut and then compacted to form the base of greens and tees. Draft animals hauled the soil about, and crews of men did the planting by hand. In today's capital-intensive world, this work is done with hydraulic machinery and earthmoving equipment. Back then, the process was labor-intensive: a sobering reminder of the craftwork and muscle power required when shaping land for golf. Initial subscriptions for the club were inadequate to cover construction costs. Crump exhausted a personal fortune to make up the deficit. He also seems to have exhausted himself, having died in 1918 with only 14 of the holes completed. The task then fell to another self-trained course designer, Hugh Wilson, who had masterminded Merion's East Course. Wilson, with the help of his brother Alan, drew upon the advice of the British designer C.H. Alison to finish holes 12 through 15 to conclude the building of Pine Valley in 1919.

Over the years, the appearance of the golf course has changed dramatically. The trees have matured and now frame every hole. Scrublands were planted with Scotch broom and laurel bushes so that the roots would hold down the sand. Some putting surfaces had to be rebuilt because the organic materials they were built upon began to rot and collapse. New greenside bunkering for several holes was required in order to forestall erosion. But despite these numerous alterations, the golf course today is, in essence, the same course that opened for play almost eighty years ago.

Superintendent Richard Christian has a crew of 19 employees year-round, 28 in summer. They have the enviable task of spending a fortune to make Pine Valley look as if it were not manicured. All the fairways are triplex mowed, all the greens and tees are hand-mowed. The tough job comes in tending the 18 acres of sand. Twice a year, the greens staff goes into the waste areas to trim bushes and scrub. Rain brings with it washouts and the need for constant repair of the hazards. Architects get a lot of credit for designing and building a layout. But when a golf course holds up for almost eighty years, it's superintendents who deserve the credit.

On every hole, the course seems in motion. Holes move laterally, left to right, right to left. Fairways twist and turn over broken ground. There are precious tracts of manicured fairway and green to cling to, with gaping wounds of earth in between.

Pine Valley moves vertically as well. At least half a dozen tee shots play over a little rise and leave you with a downhill approach shot. Three of the par-threes tumble downward. The steepest climbs are reserved for two par-fours of modest length.

The second hole, at 367 yards, unfolds straightaway through land mines of narrow sand bunkers to a green perched atop a steep rise. Only the very front of the green is visible from the fairway. When I surveyed my second shot here, I felt I had arrived just a tad too late: as if a golfer, in a desperate struggle to save himself from oblivion, had reached up from one of the bunkers fronting the green and had grabbed onto the front edge of the putting surface and pulled it down.

At Pine Valley, the slightest deviation from the proper line of play is mercilessly punished. At 6,656 yards, this par-70 course is not long. But the course is rated at 74.0, with a slope of 153! The tee shots call for forced carries over wild-looking scrub lands. Pity the golfer who cannot consistently carry the tee shot 180 yards.

In this modern age, it might not seem much to have to carry a drive that far, but to do so every time, on demand, and knowing that the requirement is not simply boldness of flight but the perfect line as well. Meander a few yards here and there and disaster looms. And what happens when a golfer stands at, say, the 388 yard par-four sixth and turns away from the safer left side and elects, instead, to bite off the dogleg by driving his tee shot over the cavernous hollow? This is a shot of a very different order. The slightest fade into the prevailing wind (we almost forgot about the prevailing wind!) will bring forth that familiar wave of farewell from the caddie as the ball crashes down the embankment.

There is no letup at Pine Valley, not a weak hole anywhere. The 10th hole, only 143 yards, offers a fair-sized target. But come up a foot short and you become part of golfing lore. A pit bunker, sunk deep into the front wall of the green, will suck up the ball—and golfer as well. For good reason, this hazard has been named to commemorate a sort of satanic proctologist. My favorite story among the many it has spawned concerns a low-handicapper who scored a 38 on the front side, only to drive into this infernal bunker at the 10th and ring up a score of 38 for the hole.

The golfer at Pine Valley is faced with a variety of strategic courses. Indeed, the genius of the course is that it combines the terror of penal architecture with the options of the strategic school. At the 433 yard par-four 16th, for example, the golfer can choose between a modest carry off the tee to the left or a booming shot over a massive sprawling bunker. A timid shot leaves the player with an extremely long second, and to play this approach safe to the right brings into play a lake that runs along the right side of the fairway. The intrepid tee shot, by contrast, while riskier at the outset, considerably shortens the approach because the landing area here runs downhill, leaving the bold of heart with but a middle-iron to the putting surface.

Every hole, every shot at Pine Valley, etches itself in the mind of the golfer lucky enough to play there. Yes, the course has its faults. There are too many blind tee shots. Too many of the fairway bunkers are impossibly narrow to play out of. And the hazards are difficult enough without having to face the prospects of finding your golf ball in a footprint. Would it be too much to ask for bunker rakes?

But who can complain? Pine Valley is a most exacting golf course. Hit the island fairways, carry the ball to the island greens, and you have a good chance to play to your handicap. But let up for a moment, or not hit the shot perfectly, and there's every chance you'll find yourself wondering how you made that 10.

There are countless subjective factors that determine what is the best golf course. My own instinct is to resist the question. The subject does not admit of quantitative reckoning. Besides, there is too much emphasis on being No. 1. The important point is that Pine Valley stands up, almost eighty years after it opened, as a demanding yet elegant test of golf. There is no truer test of a golf course than that on the way home after a round, you can visualize every shot, every vista, every hole you have played.

Augusta National: What You See and What You Don't See

The Masters is the most-watched golf event of the year. For those of us who stay at home and follow the tournament on television, there's a lot we see that's unique about the layout, as well as much we never see at all. Here's a viewer's guide.

See: A perfectly manicured golf course, the fairways mowed in stripes, every blade of grass impeccable, and pure blazing white sand bunkers. Hey, why can't my golf course look like that?

Don't See: Augusta National's maintenance budget, which is next only to the CIA's allotment as a closely-guarded state secret. Half the year the layout is closed: plastic liners are placed over the bunkers to prevent contamination, and permeable cloth tents are erected over some of the greens in summer to shade putting surfaces. The green at the 12th hole has underground pipes for both refrigeration and heating.

See: Greens so frighteningly quick—and contoured as well—that at times players are just trying to avoid three-putting. Mark Hayes once faced a downhill, four-foot birdie putt on the 18th, and took a six for the hole. His third putt was from 40 feet!

Don't See: As fast as the putting surfaces are, they'd be worse except that virtually all of them have been softened over the years to accommodate faster putting speeds. The greens, averaging 6,000 square feet in size, used to contain areas for pins that sloped 4.5 to 6 percent (measured in vertical drop per 100 feet horizontally). No set of greens at any tournament course in the world are more continually adjusted and refined. In 1994-1995, slopes at the 3rd, 4th, and 17th were softened down to about 3.5 percent from 4 to 4.5.

See: A golf course designed by Alister MacKenzie and Bobby Jones.

Don't See: Little remains of MacKenzie's trademark bunker styling. MacKenzie never designed a symmetrically curved bunker in his life, and the original Augusta National sported all manner of jagged-edged bunkers. Literally, the only remaining untouched MacKenzie bunker on the golf course today is the escalloped fairway trap on the 10th hole short of the green, and even this used to be greenside until Perry Maxwell moved the putting surface 40 yards back and left in 1937. Well over a dozen architects have subsequently had their hand in various aspects of tweaking and redesign, with the result that the bunker styling has been rounded off and kidney-shaped, with something lost in the process. The worst-renovated bunkers are the Nicklaus-designed fairway complex on the 360-yard third hole. Their placement totally eliminates the original strategic option of playing it down the left side.

See: A very solid routing that makes excellent use of the 365-acre former nursery on which the golf course sits.

Don't See: The original routing has held up, with some very interesting alterations. The nines were reversed after the first Masters, in large measure because the current front nine is on higher ground and dried out earlier than the lower-lying back nine. It thus made for earlier starting times, and for a more exciting finish. The current seventh green is 30 yards behind and above the original green. The 11th hole used to be an indifferent and much shorter par-four that doglegged right. The 16th used to be a shorter par-three that went from right of the current 15th green diagonally across the creek, until Robert Trent Jones built the present hole in 1947 into one of the game's most dramatic amphitheater par-threes.

See: Towering pines framing every hole.

Don't See: Hardwoods. Longtime club patriarch Clifford Roberts hated to look for his golf ball under leaves, so he had all the deciduous trees removed.

See: Go-for-broke excitement at the 485-yard par-five 13th hole.

Don't See: Players—a la Tommy Nakajima in 1978—opting to hit the ball out of the grassy creek fronting the green. It used to be possible, until the stream bed was rebuilt and given a clean straight edge and the water level raised. Wouldn't it be great to restore that alternative? In 1996, the water level was dropped, allowing for somewhat more flexibility, but the edge is still too steeply contoured to hold the ball up as well as it used to.

See: A colorful golf course, with diverse flowering shrubs.

Don't See: The scale of the place, both horizontally and vertically. TV cameras condense depth and dimension, while a home screen can't convey any sense of space or place. The first time you head out onto the golf course from the clubhouse, you are overwhelmed by the size of the golf course. Everyone has the same feeling—how enormous the fairways are, and how boldly the ground rises and falls. The 10th fairway seems to tumble off the edge of the world, while the 18th seemingly climbs straight uphill off the tee.

Speaking of Hills

First-time visitors to Augusta National Golf Club are always stunned by the scale of the grounds. Here, after all, is a layout with breathtaking elevation changes: 173 feet in all.

At times, the fairways look akin to wild slopes. The 10th

hole alone tumbles 106 feet, turning a 485-yard par-four into a drive and pitch for modern professionals. Of course, a basic rule of the land is that for every foot traveled downhill, you have to make up for it with a foot uphill somewhere else. That's why the 18th hole seems to climb straight up to the sky; it is, after all, routed adjacent to the downhill 10th, but runs in the opposite direction. Small wonder that when Tom Weiskopf first played Augusta National, he called it "one of the hilliest courses I had ever seen."

Normally, characterizing a golf course as "hilly" is the kiss of death. It is notoriously difficult to route a layout over steep terrain. But then, few courses sitting on such rolling ground have been routed with more genius and skill than Augusta National. Co-designers Robert Tyre Jones, Jr. and Dr. Alister MacKenzie brilliantly utilized the 365-acre Fruitlands Nursery site. In a 1932 article called "Plans for the Ideal Golf Course," MacKenzie, writing about the property that was to become Augusta National, said "Although undulating, it is not hilly." Perhaps a more accurate account on his part would have been that the routing maximizes on-site elevation change without appearing to be contrived or unreasonable.

A golf course architect today working on the same site would surely employ sophisticated of earthmoving equipment to soften some of the elevation changes by shifting dirt from higher to lower ground. Classical architects were not so lucky. Or perhaps we should say they were not so handicapped. Instead of relying upon bulldozers, they used their imaginations.

The standard way of dealing with a hilly site is to route as many holes as possible downhill and save the uphill treks for the walks from green to tee. That often requires lengthy hikes between holes, something MacKenzie abhorred. On the contrary, the walks between holes at Augusta National are very short, and at no point does the elevation change from green to tee exceed nine feet (16th green to 17th tee). On this course, golfers play the elevation changes rather than walk between them.

The key to Augusta National is that the tees were placed on natural rises, often overlooking dramatic falloffs, and then the fairway sat on ground midway in terms of elevation change to the green, which was always sited on either a natural plateau or hollow. A perfect example comes at the first hole, where the perched tee on this 400-yard par-four is 27 feet above a fall-away right in front of the fairway. The landing area for the tee shot is actually nine feet above the teeing ground, but the feel of this opening drive is less severe because the shot carries across so much open ground.

Many of the par-four holes at Augusta National play uphill from an elevated tee. The theme of the first hole is reprised at the 3rd, 5th, 7th, 17th, and 18th holes, and nowhere is the effect more dramatic than at the concluding fairway. Here on this 405-yard par-four, the golfer faces a drive that seems to play into a natural wall. In fact, the fairway landing area is only 20 feet above the teeing ground, but the effect is magnified since the ground gives way in front of the tee and then rises 32 feet from the low point. From mid-fairway, the second shot must climb another 36 feet to the putting surface. Such an uphill slope makes a 170-yard approach shot play more than a full club longer.

When it comes to uphill climbs at Augusta National, nothing surpasses the par-five eighth hole. The tee shot on this 535-yard hole rises only five feet, but from the mid-fairway bunker in the landing area to the green, the ground climbs 62 feet! Ascents of more than 30 feet on a hole are rare in contemporary design. When faced with a steep uphill, most designers would prefer to scalp the hill somewhat and nudge the material down to level off the elevations. At Augusta National's eighth hole, the green cannot be glimpsed from mid-fairway, but Jones and MacKenzie built a little knob just below the peak of the hill that allows players to orient their second shot.

Ben Crenshaw, 1995 Masters champion and a prominent course designer in his own right, points out that what makes the steep topography of Augusta National playable "is that all of the edges and slopes have been softened so that despite its severity, it has a gentle look and feel."

On uphill holes, golfers who hit the ball on a higher trajectory have a tremendous advantage over players who launch the ball at a lower angle. On approach shots at the seventh hole (a 20-foot rise), for instance, the higher trajectory does not hit the hill as fast and so comes down softer, with more control.

On downhill shots, by contrast, the advantage normally goes to the low ball hitter, since his shot descends at a softer angle and thus takes better advantage of the slope. And what more dramatic downhill holes than the long holes at Augusta National? The par-five second falls off 96 feet. No wonder modern tournament golfers regularly reach this 555-yard hole with long-irons for their second shot.

The routing of Augusta National is particularly ingenious in how the downhill fairway slopes are designed to reward the long hitter. A classic case comes at the 10th hole, where the fairway grade intensifies some 255 yards off the back tee. The golfer who can carry his tee shot this far enjoys the benefit of a generous "kick point" and ends up dozens of yards ahead of the player who carries the ball only 240 yards. The same effect at the 500-yard par-five 15th hole helps spread the field between short hitters and those who can carry the crest of the hill 240 yards from the tee. That's why Ben Crenshaw hit four-wood to the green the final day in 1995 while Tiger Woods, who carries his drive much further, was able to hit but an eight-iron.

There is no more dramatic shot in golf than a long downhill approach over water. The ball seemingly hang-glides forever, and it isn't always easy to guesstimate how much more yardage the downslope provides. The exact formula for such a calculation is what is known as a differential equation, and it takes into account such factors as yardage, vertical drop, velocity, trajectory and spin rate of the golf ball. The subject was complicated enough to merit scrutiny by a panel of experts at the Second World Scientific Congress of Golf held in St. Andrews in 1994. What does this mean for the player who is standing 235 yards out from the 15th green, with the putting surface 36 feet below him, and he's out there sweating away without benefit of a Ph.D. in mathematics? According to mechanical engineer Michael Twiggs, manager of technical development at True Temper Sports in Memphis, "the shot will play like 225."

On downhill shots, a lower trajectory will yield longer distance. But precisely the problem with low-slung shots is that once on the ground, they tend to run, and thus are harder to keep to an intended target. At Augusta National, position around the greens is everything, and it's especially important to land the ball as softly as possible to specific points. Once again, then, advantage goes to the high-ball hitter.

The fairways are not the only features with dramatic vertical slopes. Although Augusta National's putting surfaces have been softened, they are still among the most steeply contoured in golf. Consider the green at the 405-yard par-four 14th. The hole climbs 30 feet on a steady grade from tee to putting surface, and there's not a bunker to be found anywhere. But who needs a hazard when the green itself slopes 7 feet 4 inches from the mound in the back left center to the shelf up front? By way of comparison, this one putting surface has more elevation change than does all of Harbour Town Golf Links!

The ninth green also slopes 7 feet 4 inches from back to front. When viewed from the fairway 30 feet below, the putting surface looks like it is about to slide off the hillside.

Up and down the slippery slope. That's the name of the game at Augusta National. The course has the fastest greens, the most beautiful flora, and also some of the most amazing elevation changes in all of tournament golf.

Note: Vertical elevation change at Augusta National GC measures 173 feet. The high point (elevation 337′) is just behind the first green. The low point (elevation 164′) is at the 12th fairway fronting Rae's Creek. When it comes to natural slope, Augusta National stands up well to other highly rated layouts.

Harbour Town GL, 4 ft.
Oak Hill CC-East Course, 42 ft.
Oakmont CC, 47 ft.
Pinehurst CC-No. 2, 50 ft.
The Country Club, 50 ft.
Pine Valley GC, 54 ft.
Winged Foot CC-West Course, 62 ft.
Merion GC-East Course, 67 ft.
Oakland Hills CC-South Course, 70 ft.

Pebble Beach GC, 88 ft.
Wade Hampton GC, 110 ft.
Muirfield Village GC, 115 ft.
Riviera CC, 117 ft.
Cypress Point GC, 118 ft.
Shinnecock Hills GC, 120 ft.
Shadow Creek GC, 213 ft.
Cascades GC, 230 ft.

CO

East Lake: The Heart and Soul of a New Atlanta

Fourteen-year-old Maurice Ogeubhi had seen some golf on television, but it took a presentation in his school about caddying to get him thinking seriously about the game. He listened carefully as Trey Cassell and Lance Olson, representatives of a nearby golf club, explained the kind of work that was available there. Anyone interested in making money? Outdoors? If so, training was available.

Maurice now has a job: weekends, and then when school's out, he hopes to loop every day. No need to hang out all day waiting for work. The system is simple: caddies call in at night, and if they have an assigned loop the next day, they show up an hour before tee time.

The pay is $20-25 per bag, plus a tip. The fee is arranged through the club, and every two weeks Maurice has a paycheck awaiting him. Plus, he's learning the game, an education that includes a chance to play the course on Mondays.

Welcome to East Lake Golf Club, the heart and soul of an Atlanta neighborhood in the process of rebuilding. The site is exactly five miles east of downtown Atlanta, in the midst of a partially run-down residential area adjacent to one of the city's more troubled public housing tracts. But it wasn't always thus.

In 1908, the Atlanta Athletic Club built a golf course on wooded parkland at what was then the outer reaches of an electric streetcar line. The original layout by Tom Bendelow assumed its current routing in 1913 through the work of Donald Ross. In 1959, George Cobb performed a clumsy "modernization" of the layout in preparation for the 1963 Ryder Cup matches. Thankfully, Rees Jones has just completed a masterful reconstruction of the golf course to its former luster, and then some.

East Lake enjoys a glorious history, in large measure because for many years it was the home course of Bobby Jones, whose family spent summers in a cottage on the course. Jones shared this wonderful golf ground with a legendary crew that included Scottish-born head pro Stewart Maiden and two golfers Charlie Yates and Alexa Stirling, who as contemporaries of Jones also won numerous amateur championships. In its heyday, the Atlanta Athletic Club comprised two courses.

Gradually, however, the club's fortunes waned, in large part because of the same economic and demographic factors—collectively known as "white flight"—that have afflicted almost every other American city. The golf courses remained busy, but use of the club's dining and other social facilities slowed down as members feared venturing through the nearby streets to reach the club.

Many members pressed for a wholly new facility on the north side of Atlanta, closer to the areas of rapid suburban growth and away from the perceived troubles of the East Lake neighborhood. In an emotionally contentious decision in 1966, the AAC sold off the second golf course and applied the proceeds as down payment on a new 600-acre site along the Chattahoochee River in Duluth, Georgia.

The remaining course became part of a newly formed East Lake Golf Club. Across the street, on the land where the second layout once stood, sprawled one of those ridiculously ill-conceived housing projects of the 1960s: 650 low-income units stuffed onto a 55-acre parcel. Not surprisingly, East Lake Meadows, as it was dubbed, soon became a shooting gallery, a crack cocaine distribution center that further contributed to the area's decline. Sadly but inevitably, East Lake Golf Club followed in its wake.

Then came Tom Cousins in 1993. Cousins, born in 1933, long has been one of Atlanta's premier real estate developers. In the 1950s he started out by selling prefab housing units. Gradually, he expanded into commercial and residential real estate. When the regional market suffered a disastrous bust in the early 1970s, he was one of the few survivors. Cousins then oversaw development of the Omni Arena downtown and helped lure the NBA's Hawks and the NHL's Flames to town.

More recently, he set out to salvage East Lake. Under the

aegis of the East Lake Community Foundation, a subsidiary of his own C.F. Foundation, Cousins proposed a partnership with the federal government's Housing and Urban Development agency (HUD) and private developers to invest about $100 million to rehabilitate the golf course and the surrounding community.

Among the many intelligent things Cousins did was to hire Rees Jones as his golf course architect. True to form, Jones' work on East Lake has been magical. Whatever charm the older incarnations of the golf course may have had, this version is simply stunning. Strictly speaking, this was not a pure restoration, because Ross' version of the golf course used to have double greens on each hole—one for winter, one for summer. By the 1950s the greens had been unified, but in relying upon old aerial and ground photography—there were no detailed Ross maps or blueprints—Jones had to make decisions about re-siting greens and adding contours.

Along the way, he stripped the course, reworked the slopes, reconstructed every bunker, put in new irrigation and drainage, and then sodded the fairways. The only significant routing tweak was swinging the old 17th fairway and green to the left so that they now sit astride the shore of 27-acre East Lake.

Everything is now in place: a brilliant old peninsula green par-three that juts out into the lake; a short, dogleg par-four with a fairway crevice that used to be a Civil War bunker; two stunning short par-fives on the back nine with strategic bunkers in the second-shot landing area; and a heart-stopping 232-yard par-three final hole over water and yawning front bunkers. With East Lake, it's as if a rusty old 12-cylinder Bugatti touring car that had been languishing in the barn has been newly outfitted, polished, and made road-ready.

Director of golf Jim Gerber explains that Rees Jones "left his mark here by not leaving his mark." Golfers familiar with his trademark chocolate drop containment mounding will find none of it here. Much of the credit also goes to project manager Mike O'Shea, who rebuilt the course and so impressed Cousins that he was hired away from the contractor, Landscapes Unlimited, to become East Lake's superintendent.

Interns from Mississippi State, Penn State, and Georgia State lend a hand on the agronomy and golf staffs. There's also that well-trained crew of caddies—all 370 of them. To encourage walking, the cart paths have been taken out, and of the three motorized carts available to medically excused members, none has a bag strap.

Meticulous care was taken in restoring the slate-roof and brick-exterior English Tudor clubhouse (one of whose chimneys once was toppled by a lightning strike and nearly ended the career and life of Bobby Jones). Fully 38,000 square feet of ramshackle additions were removed, and the remaining original 40,000 square feet were restored into a living golf museum that includes Bobby Jones' old double locker, now on display in the pro shop. With the club now focused on golf, the old tennis courts were ripped up, the pool demolished, and the minuscule boat club scuttled.

Cousins' plans are equally ambitious for the neighborhood. The East Lake Foundation will spend about $60 million on a 175-acre parcel across the street, of which 95 acres will be donated by the Foundation, 25 by the city of Atlanta, and 55 acres from East Lake Meadows. The housing project will be torn down and replaced with 500 units, 50 percent federally subsidized and the other 50 percent available for rent or purchase at market rates. On the grounds of the long-neglected second golf course, Jones is designing a 4,300-yard, par-63 public golf course with a teaching academy. Walking will be vigorously encouraged, with caddie fees subsidized by the club, and superior loopers "graduating" to the championship course across the street.

Championship, indeed. East Lake, a participant in the Western Golf Association and its Evans Caddie Scholarship Fund, has already secured the 1997 Western Junior, the 1998 PGA Tour Championship, the U.S. Amateur in 2001, and the Southern Amateur in 2002—the year of Bobby Jones' centenary. Don't be surprised if East Lake also lands the Ryder Cup in 2003 and a U.S. Open soon thereafter.

None of this comes cheap. But the social costs of neglecting the life of a community are expensive, too. Atlanta's corporate powers have come through in an impressive way, in part with job opportunities for area residents, in part through memberships.

Club memberships, available to CEOs of socially conscious Fortune 500 companies, cost $50,000, plus a minimum $200,000 donation to the East Lake Community Foundation. For this, the member gets to prepay 200 rounds a year at $125 per round, plus pay annual dues and caddie fees.

The luckiest people in the whole equation just might be the members of the old East Lake club, who held on throughout the dramatic transition.

Or is it residents of the East Lake neighborhood who consider themselves even more blessed? One thing's for sure. Maurice Ogeubhi has a job. He also has big plans to become an electrical engineer. It just might be golf that helps him get there.

⚭

Bethpage Black

When the registration desk at Bethpage State Park on Long Island opened at 4 a.m. on a Sunday morning in May, 400 people were lined up for tee times. They had started their wait at dusk the night before. By 7 a.m. that morning, the waiting time to tee off had reached four hours for each of Bethpage's five 18-hole layouts.

This is a true public facility, and now it's slated to host the 2002 U.S. Open. Wouldn't it be fitting for the world's best players to overnight in their courtesy cars for the week?

Three cheers to New York State's Office of Parks, Recreation, and Historic Preservation for making quality public golf available for only $20-$25 per round. The entire facility owes its existence to the Depression-era efforts of metropolitan visionary Robert Moses. Perhaps the world's most ambitious land planner, he put thousands of people to work for the government in creating the bridges, tunnels, highways, beaches, and parks that shaped the New York area.

Among those whom Moses had the good sense to hire was a down-on-his-luck New York-based golf architect named A.W. Tillinghast. The creator of such gems as Winged Foot and Baltimore's Five Farms ended his design career with Bethpage Black in 1935.

For years, the course enjoyed a fine reputation as one of the region's most demanding challenges and as a fitting site for professional tournaments. It sat high atop many national ranking lists, but as budgetary constraints took their toll, the course badly deteriorated. That is, until the middle 1980s, when park superintendent Jim Evans arrived on board and began overseeing a meticulous renovation and upgrading program. Today, the course bears all the trademarks of "Terrible Tillie" at his best.

The par-71 course plays 6,556 yards, with a slope of 131 and a rating of 70.5. And those are the forward tees! At tournament time the course can be stretched to 7,065 yards, slope 144/rating 75.4.

The holes are cut through dark woods and low, snarly scrub. With 46,000 rounds a year played on the course, rounds can often take six hours. One effort to speed up play has been to discourage high-handicappers and to direct them to the other four courses at Bethpage. As for riding Bethpage Black, forget it. Carts are simply prohibited. A golfer not prepared to trek some very steep terrain is best advised to avoid this course.

For too long, public golfers in this country have been treated to insultingly boring courses. Hazards were taken out of the right side to speed play along. Sprinkler heads on the greens facilitated maintenance but interfered with putting. Sand bunkers were flattened down instead of being flashed up and boldly presented. Greens sized 9,000 square feet became standard practice, and whatever contours they may have had were obliterated through indifferent patterns of ride-mowing.

The beauty of a public facility like Bethpage Black is that it shows respect for the public golfer's intelligence. Strategic options prevail. The bunkering is at times severe, but there's always a safe path allowed.

At the 424-yard fifth hole, for instance, golfers at the elevated tee contemplate a forbidding elongated bunker that snakes in diagonally down the right side of the driving area. There's bail-out room to the left, and a chance for the crack player to carry the hazard altogether. The very next hole, a 391-yard dogleg left, presents a completely different challenge: a trio of potted sand hazards traverses the near side of the driving area. This time, the safe shot is to the right, while the bold drive toward left center will catch the downhill and leave but a short-iron to the green.

When Tillinghast built Bethpage Black, some earthmoving equipment was deployed, but nothing on a modern scale. The result is a course whose contours naturally fit in with the existing terrain. One of the virtues of soil greens, as opposed to the modern, suspended water-table putting surfaces which conform to USGA specifications, is that the older greens required less work and could more readily be made to complement natural contour lines. At Bethpage, Tillinghast simply placed his greens on knobs of hills or at the front edge of a plateau and then scalloped out some bunkers around the edge. By the way, for the 2002 U.S. Open, plans call for some lengthening of holes and restoring several abandoned bunkers. The original green surfaces will be left structurally untouched and need only to be restored to their initial size of about 4,000 square feet, some 20 percent larger than they are today.

Tillinghast built some of the most imaginative bunkering to be seen in golf. He was not afraid to display sand, and his hazards sport a raw, fleshy look, as if the bunkers were natural scars in the earth which he wished simply to highlight. There is no need to apologize for a golf course that is difficult. But the beauty of a strategic course such as Bethpage Black is that the thinking golfer can find a way around without having to hit all-or-nothing shots on each hole. The only problem is that when you've camped out half the night to play, you're not in the best frame of mind to play.

But that doesn't deter golfers in the New York metropolitan area. And when it comes to great golf, snobbery gives way real fast. Monday is the busiest day at Bethpage Black. That's when Long Island's private clubs are closed. The blue bloods know a good deal. The spirit of public golf is alive and well at Bethpage Black. The minute the last putt drops at the 2002 Open, folks will be camping out in the parking lot.

Oakland Hills: Interview with "A Monster"

by Dr. B.S. Shrink, MBA, DQ, Ph.D., OB

Oakland Hills CC-South Course, site of the 1996 U.S. Open, is known as "The Monster." But it wasn't always that way, as the following candid interview makes clear.

Monster: I've lived with this stupid name for 45 years now and I'm sick of it.

Dr.: What do you mean?

Monster: I was brought into this world in 1916 to give pleasure to people. My father, Donald Ross, was a gentle man, maybe a little tight-fisted, arrogant, too, but that's the only way he could get his work done without having everyone tell him what to do. He worked hard getting things right, and early on, everything was soft and gentle, no hard edges, nothing severe. nothing scary or frightening. I was pleased with how I looked and didn't have to hide under tree cover or anything. Then it happened, when I was 21, and I can hardly admit to talking about it at all.

Dr.: Then what happened?

Monster: It was 1937, about 150 men stayed here for three days and played, and one of them, Ralph Guldahl, he really had his way with me, scored big-time, seven-under.

Dr.: But the May 1996 issue of *USGA Golf Journal* reports that "Only one Open champion, Andy North, has ever won there with an under-par total."

Monster: The report is wrong. Guldahl scored 281. Back then I played to a par-72. It's all a USGA cover-up. That's probably why Guldahl disappeared a few years later. I figure someone got to him and . . . well, you can fill in the rest.

Dr. And you?

Monster: Like it was my fault? People were embarrassed for me, as if they had to make excuses. Blaming the victim and all that stuff. Then the war came, and everything was quiet, folks didn't build cars here in town and the executives didn't come out all that much since we were so far out of town, what with the gasoline restrictions and all. I figured the whole incident was forgotten. Then next thing you know, the Cold War is on, and then some guy in a fedora shows up and starts digging around.

Dr.: Fedora?

Monster: Calls himself Mr. Jones. Some alias. Starts walking around, checking all kinds of maps, taking shots at me.

Dr.: Can you prove this?

Monster: Prove it? I got a suitcase full of cocktail napkins with his doodlings on them. I'm still thinking of pressing charges. Anyway, he wouldn't leave me alone, kept scratching at me, pawing, pulling, then next thing I know he's at me with bulldozers and he's like doing major surgery. Not that he changed any of my arteries or organs. But still, he sliced my guts up pretty good and then put me back together all again. I recovered, but I felt different. I used to be inviting, would encourage people to spend time here, and I wouldn't slap them down if their approach was a little awkward. All that changed. It's like someone gave me nasty pills, started smacking people down if they got out of line just the slightest.

Dr.: Does anybody else know about this?

Monster: Here's the crazy part. The whole world knows about it. Some guy named Herb got Wind of it and wrote it up in some snooty East Coast magazine and then this guy Jones—man, you'd think by now he'd use his real name—this guy Jones starts bragging about it all, like he's the one who made me or something. This Mr. Jones, you could spot him because he always wore a Trent coat—he starts calling me a Monster and . . . and . . . wait a minute . . there was . . .

Dr.: Yes?

Monster: Come to think about it, there was somebody else. Higgen, Hagen, Hogan? Something like that. Started swearing at me 'cause things were getting real rough. This was right around the time all those guys with long-sleeve white shirts were here, yeah, that must have been 1951, I can remember because I had just turned 35 and, well, then all these guys came back for another three days.

Dr.: The same men who had been there in 1937?

Monster: Well, some of them were the same, most of them were different, but the really big change was that they had all sorts of different weapons.

Dr.: Weapons?

Monster: Didn't I tell you about the weapons? The tools, whatever. When I was young they used wooden sticks and they'd slap around these sort of round balls with these weird swings, like they were throwing their arms around their bodies. Then things started changing. The wood disappeared, they started using metal sticks, and the balls, they started getting white and real round. Plus they looked different when they swung, like they had taken vitamins or something, because those balls were traveling a lot higher and farther. But the biggest difference is that they used to get all caught up in these big ugly scars in my skin, but over the years, they started using a heavy metal tool—looks like a rake or something—and then they had no trouble with my scars. That's when my boss—his name was Oswald, no, not that Oswald—anyway, they used to call him green chairman, John Oswald was his name, and he started getting worried, like I couldn't even defend myself. And that's when he called in that Mr. Jones, and next thing you know, he moved all those scars around—man, did that ever hurt—and then in that year, 1951, I guess, those guys couldn't have their way with me anymore. That's when they started calling me Monster. Oh, it hurts so much just to . . sob . . . sob . . . I'm sorry.

Dr.: What hurts?

Monster: I'm not a monster, that's what; why do they call me that? And that Mr. Jones, people talk about him like he was the one who made me what I am. I mean, I don't know if I blame him, because all these guys with note pads and tape recorders who walk around here eating free sandwiches—they must be gypsies, and they spend all this time under a tent when everybody else is outdoors—well, anyway, they wrote all this stuff about Jones and Trent and Monsters and then the next thing you know folks are acting like I'm his. They talk about that big lake on my backside as if he put it there. That was there all along. You know, I got a call three years ago.

Dr.: A call?

Monster: Yeah, from a Mr. Baltus Rol, and he told me a real similar story, only his dad was a Mr. Tillie, not Ross, but it had to do with a water hole, only this one was on his front side.

Dr.: Front side of Mr. Baltus Rol? Carry forth.

Monster: Yeah, and it turns out that our Mr. Jones was out there too, right after he got done with me, and there was an old watering hole there in front of the clubhouse, and next thing you know folks are making like it was Mr. Jones who put it there when it turns out Mr. Tillie had put it there years before.

Dr.: Very interesting.

Monster: Anyway, I'm all confused, because I can't even tell anymore who I am. And this week, all them people are going to back out on top of me, and there'll be all this talk, and Mr. Jones and all, and I'm all scared because if they have their way with me again and people will blame me and . . . . sob . . . sob . . . well, what am I supposed to do?

Dr.: Look, growing up and maturing are things we all have to go through. You've had to make a tougher adjustment than most, because a lot of the changes were forced upon you. But you know, for an 80-year old monster you're in pretty good shape and everybody loves to visit with you and tell you old stories.

Monster: That's easy for you to say, but I still miss those days before everything got complicated.

Dr.: Just try to be yourself.

Monster: But which one?

Dr.: Uh-oh, our 50 minutes are up. See you in ten years.

10

Best and Worst Awards

Best and Worst Awards

We suffer from a tyranny of lists: top-100, best public, best new resort for left-handers. It seems that if a developer's course doesn't make one of these lists he sues the architect for malpractice. The proliferation of these creates too much hype and puts designers in a position where their major concern is to come up with something sexy for opening day. After that, they can forget about playability and leave the maintenance nightmare to overworked superintendents.

With the emphasis on courses by marquee-name architects, and with all the new top-dollar venues opening up, too much attention is paid to the latest and the most expensive, and not enough attention paid to basic elements of sound design.

Field reports derived from my committee of one have now been collated. Forget about any claims of objectivity. Nor was the following list tabulated by some high-priced accounting firm. So here's one version of what these lists really ought to look like.

CROSSOVER SHOT AWARD: The par-five 18th at Lahinch in Ireland calls for a drive that cuts perpendicular to the fifth and sixth holes. Since the present routing was created in 1928, no one has been hit.

HACK-ARTIST AWARD: The holes built by George and Tom Fazio at Inverness in Toledo, Ohio, prior to the 1979 Open still do not fit. The new par-four fifth hole looks like a car park despite every decent effort by architect/member Arthur Hills to compensate.

BEST REMODELING JOB: The Country Club, Brookline, Massachusetts. This restoration for the 1988 U.S. Open did more to generate popular appreciation for classical course design than any single course project in recent golf history. It undid much of the clumsy work done earlier and redeemed the legendary par-four 17th as one of the country's most distinctive doglegs. The pros at the '88 Open loved it, and the work lifted Rees Jones into national prominence.

SHOUT IT FROM THE MOUNTAIN-TOP AWARD: Sugarloaf, Carrabassett Valley, Maine, by Robert Trent Jones, Jr. The view from the tee at the par-three 11th, nearly 200 feet above the Carrabassett River, with 4,350-foot Mount Sugarloaf to the right, is simply overwhelming.

WORST SHOT IN GOLF: Tee shot at the par-four eighth at Pebble Beach, Monterey, California. There's nothing to see except the steeply rising wall of rough that blocks out the fairway. But nobody cares, because . . . .

BEST SHOT IN GOLF: Approach to the green at the par-four eighth at Pebble Beach, Monterey, California. A few unfortunate souls have driven their golf carts off the cliff while in awe of this splendid view.

MOST UNUSUAL STRETCH OF HOLES: The canyon holes, Nos. 13 through 17, at Black Diamond Ranch, Lecanto, Florida. Tom Fazio always puts the serious trouble on the left side, but this time he outdid himself. Hook the ball off the tee at the par-five 14th and your ball touches down in a vast watery pit where dinosaurs roam.

MOST UNDERRATED ARCHITECT OF THE CENTURY: George C. Thomas, Jr. did Riviera, Bel Air, and Los Angeles CC North, wrote the most riveting (and obscure) of all architecture books in 1927, then quit the business entirely.

MOST REGRETTABLE ADDITIONS TO GOLF COURSES: Cart paths, symmetrically-shaped trees for 150-yard markers, ornamental flower beds, lakes with fountains, wire mesh fences, and interior O.B. stakes, heavy-handed hole signage, and advertising at the bottom of the cup.

SOMETIMES YOU GOTTA BREAK THE RULES: Forget about "design balance." Cypress Point, Pebble Beach, California, has consecutive par-fives, consecutive short par-fours, and consecutive par-threes. Runner-up, Inwood CC, Inwood, Long Island, site of Bobby Jones' 1923 U.S. Open victory, has three consecutive par-fives on the front nine.

MOST ELEGANT FAIRWAY BUNKER: The trap in the middle of the 10th hole at Augusta National, Augusta, Georgia, is the only feature originally designed by Alister MacKenzie still left on the course.

BEST NINE HOLE COURSE: Whitinsville Golf Club, Whitinsville, Massachusetts. A pure gem of an old Donald Ross design with a creaky wooden clubhouse and fescue-framed holes that brilliantly snuggle into the site.

MOST HISTORICAL GOLF COURSE: The National Golf Links, Southampton, Long Island, New York. This 1909 museum piece by Charles Blair Macdonald first showed America the craft of course design.

BROKE THE MOLD AWARD: Harbour Town, Hilton Head, South Carolina, by Pete Dye (1969) repudiated modern trends of length and power. There can't be five feet of elevation change on this site, yet Pete managed to create visually interesting features and shot-making variety. Too bad the ownership has milked it to near-death by overpricing and overcrowding.

GOOFIEST MODERN GREEN: The par-four fourth hole at Spyglass Hill, Monterey, California. Robert Trent Jones, Sr. must have forgotten to unfold the grading plan when building this wafer-thin, elongated green.

WORST COURSE HOSTING A MAJOR EVENT: The Belfry, Sutton Coldfield, England, site of the Ryder Cup in 1985-89-93-2001 has been an embarrassment to international golf. Looks like a Florida muni sitting on a potato field. Short little par-four 10th is memorable only as a joke.

MOST FASCINATING SEASIDE COURSE: The Old Course, St. Andrews. Only 11 greens, fairways 120 yards wide, you can drive the ball left all day long (except at No. 9 and No. 10) and still be in fairway. If a modern architect created this treeless moonscape he'd be drummed out of the business as an incompetent. Forget your first impression. Each hole can be played five different ways. And what better setting for a final green than the town square of a medieval university town?

DUSTY OLD GEM AWARD: Cranwell GC, Lenox, Massachusetts. Eleven original holes from Wayne Stiles and John Van Kleek's 1926 design remain today. Superintendent Karl Baumann has already done miracles on a minuscule maintenance budget.

MOST UNUSUAL GREEN SITE: 13th at North Berwick, West Course, North Berwick, Scotland. The green at this short par-four sits along the rocky bank of the Firth of Forth, just on the other side of a stone wall traversing the fairway.

LOST AND FOUND AWARD: Malone CC, Malone, New York (50 miles north of Lake Placid!). The front nine on the East Course was designed and built in 1938 by Willard G. Wilkinson and includes a fabulous Redan, a roller coaster short par-five, and pure links-style bunkering.

BIGGEST INTERNATIONAL DISAPPOINTMENT: Royal Selangor, Kuala Lumpur, Malaysia. By far the least interesting of all the courses written up in *The World Atlas of Golf*.

BEST UPHILL THREE-PAR: 15th, Kingston Heath GC, Melbourne, Australia. Des Soutar routed the course, Alister MacKenzie did the greens and bunkering. The toughest achievement in design is the up-hill par-three. The plateau green complex at this 156-yard 15th boldly presents itself to the golfer.

WORST EXCESS: The floating green three-par at Coeur d'Alene, Idaho.

BEST GOLFING STATE: Minnesota. There must be more golfers than cows up there.

"WHERE'S THE BEEF?" AWARD: The Gary Player Design Group. After some 65 courses, none has made a mark. His new "signature" course at Lyman Orchards in Middlefield, Connecticut is so bad that within two years of opening in mid-1994 its two most unplayable holes (No. 6, No. 8) were slated for wholesale elimination.

BEST IDEAS IN DESIGN: Contoured bunker floors; cart paths partially hidden behind mounds; forward tees angled and staggered for different lines of play; zoysia grass fairways; fescue rough; directional bunkers; "no hunting" signs in wetlands.

WORST INNOVATIONS: Stimpmeters; yardage booklets; red, white, and blue distance dots in the fairway; "signature" golf holes; laser yardage markers on carts; memorial tree plantings; metal woods.

BEST SETTING FOR LATE AFTERNOON GOLF: Machrihanish GC, Cambletown, Scotland. At the base of the Kintyre Peninsula, with Northern Ireland visible just across the sea. The course runs along the beach, through the dunes, and back to a tiny village, with golden hills looming to the east.

WORST FAIRWAY BUNKERS: 18th hole, Melrose GC, Daufuskie Island, South Carolina. Jack Nicklaus wasted a good seaside setting with a bunker complex on this par-five that looks likes a skin graft from the Elephant Man.

BEST FAIRWAY BUNKERING: San Francisco GC, San Francisco, California. A.W. Tillinghast's 1915 sculpting has been meticulously preserved.

WORST GREENSIDE BUNKERING: Ocean Edge GC, Cape Cod, Massachusetts. Brian Silva's planet Bizarro version of "Scottish bunkering" offers hidden, teacup-sized traps, each with a dollop of sand, to greens pitched away from the line of play. It's sad to see this, especially from someone who claims to be influenced by Ross.

SANDS OF TIME AWARD: Seaside Nine at Sea Island GC, St. Simons Island, Georgia. A perfect nine-hole layout, with deceptively simple rounded greens and bunkers, designed by H.S. Colt and Charles Alison in 1928. No need to touch a thing here, what with marshlands, Intracoastal Waterway, and Atlantic Ocean providing a stunning, wind-blown setting. Attention has always rightly focused on two par-fours, the 408-yard fourth and the 424-yard seventh, for their bold bunkering. But the real stunner here is the 346-yard fifth hole, with criss-cross fairway sand and a fearsome- looking trap built into the base of the elevated green.

MOST OVERRATED RECENT MAJOR TOURNAMENT SITE: Lake Course, Olympic Club, San Francisco, California, hosted the 1955-66-87 U.S. Opens. Trees have encroached upon the fairways; there's only one fairway bunker; no water hazards; six or seven uphill approaches to greens with the same "peeping eye" bunker in the front; and a 17th tee that's 50 yards left of where it needs to be.

GOLF COURSE WHOSE STOCK HAS RISEN MOST IN A DECADE: Crystal Downs, Frankfort, Michigan. This purest of all MacKenzie designs wasn't even on the list of top-five in Michigan 10 years ago. Now it's rightly ranked among the finest 20 in the world.

CAMPUS GOLF AWARD: University Ridge, Madison, Wisconsin. Robert Trent Jones, Jr. and design associate Bruce Charlton have combined heathland and woodland in a stunningly uncomplicated design for the University of Wisconsin; construction by the Wadsworth Company.

MOST POLITICALLY CORRECT GOLF COURSE: Robert Trent Jones GC, Manassas, Virginia, 45 miles west of Washington, D.C. (i.e., against the grain of traffic). A recent standout design of Robert Trent Jones, Sr. and Roger Rulewich, with a massive clubhouse, not a house in sight, though you will have to pardon the automobile burial pit alongside the ninth tee. It hosts the President's Cup; President Clinton is a regular visitor; and it is also home to Congressmen, Supreme Court associate justices, and every other Gucci-shoed lobbyist in town.

ROCKY HORROR PICTURE SHOW AWARD: Dunmaglas, Petoskey, Michigan. This stone-age wonder designed by Larry Mancour looks like a collaborative effort of Old Tom Morris and the Acid Queen. Love those incredible disappearing fairways, wildly undulating 2,500 sq. ft. greens, and large boulders scientifically placed in the middle of landing areas—for artistic effect. So weird it deserves a cult following.

BEST HISTORICAL TOUCH: Marietta CC, Marietta, Georgia, where designer Bob Cupp incorporated existing Civil War trenchworks into the fairway contours.

AMERICAN GOTHIC AWARD: Brickyard Crossing GC, Indianapolis, Indiana. Pete Dye's total reworking of a 1928-Bill Diddel layout features four holes on the infield of the Indianapolis Motor Speedway, the grandstand for turn #3 behind the 13th green, and vistas of such American iconography as low-income houses, railroad tracks, high-tension power lines, petroleum storage gas tanks, a barn, a motel, and the wall of the old race track used to bulk up embankments along fairways. Gentlemen, start your golf swings.

BEST RESTORATION JOB: National Golf Links of America, Southampton, Long Island. Superintendent Karl Olson has been working much like an archaeologist in clearing overgrown areas and excavating Charles Blair Macdonald's long-lost bunkers. Too bad that greenside irrigation heads prevent him from expanding the greens back to their original size of some 14,000 sq. ft.

RUNAWAY BULLDOZER AWARD: TPC Valley Course at Sawgrass, Ponte Vedra, Florida. Some developer was trying to maximize lake frontage and golf course lots, so Pete Dye and Bobby Weed had about 2 million cubic yards of muck to shmear around. The result looks like a boiled-over pudding that got flash-frozen.

BEST AREA FOR PUBLIC GOLF: Northwest Montana's Flathead Valley, with eight courses, averaging about $30 green fees. Eagle Bend is the best of the lot, but the 36-holes at Whitefish Lake GC are close behind, and the new nine-hole addition to Mission Mountain CC in Ronan make for a real stunner there as well.

RIP VAN WINKLE AWARD: Gleneagles at the Equinox GC, Manchester Village, Vermont. Rees Jones' redesign awoke this 1927-Walter Travis course from a very long slumber.

HONEY, CALL THE PLUMBER AWARD: "Fuzzy's Ledge," seventh hole, Reynolds Plantation, Greensboro, Georgia. Zoeller apparently thought a greenside bunker that fell off into a pond should have about a half-inch of water covering it. Provides for interesting options, but to achieve it the lake should have an overflow valve to control the level.

BEST PURE DUNESLAND PAR-THREE: The 14th at the Maidstone Club, East Hampton, New York. The oasis-like green at this 143-yard hole is stark and stunningly beautiful.

TOWER OF POWER AWARD: Sixth hole, Indian Summer G&CC, Olympia, Washington. Can't take down massive power line towers that diagonally cross a par-four? Just split the fairway around them, and create alternative paths.

McCULLOUGH CHAINSAW AWARD: Golf architect Jerry Matthews, who has taken tree preservation to extremes at Elk Ridge GC and the Lakes Course-Michaywe in Northern Michigan. Narrow! (Kudos, however, for his "pig in a poke" bunker fronting the 10th green at Elk Ridge in honor of owner Lou Schmidt of Honey Baked Ham Company.)

DESERT ROSE AWARD: Desert Forest GC, Carefree, Arizona. Every modern architect ought to study this amazingly simple 1962 Red Laurence design. Not a fairway bunker anywhere, but who needs it with the Sonoran Desert flanking every landing area? Every green is bunkered at 4 o'clock and 8 o'clock, with the distance between sand proportional to the length of the approach shot. Best hole by far is the par-five seventh, with its optional island fairway off the tee on the right. Unlike most "alternate fairway" holes, this one really works.

IRISH-CANADIAN FRIENDSHIP AWARD: Devil's Paintbrush, Toronto, Ontario. This Michael Hurdzan-Dana Fry design is a low-key, Irish-style walk through lovely fescues and revetted pot bunkers, with stone walls alongside holes and an old-fashioned pub for a clubhouse.

LONGEST CART PATH BETWEEN HOLES: Ironhorse, West Palm Beach, Florida. The wooden bridge over wetlands from the 11th green to the 12th tee at this Arthur Hills-designed course is longer than a par-six.

MOST MEANINGLESS PHRASE IN COURSE DESIGN: "Signature-design." Usually refers to a famous golf pro's endorsement on the back of an inflated six-figure check for three half-day on-site photo opportunities, a cocktail party with the first 50 lot owners, and an opening tee shot: "Hey, where does this hole go?" A sure sign is the video sales pitch, replete with the "designer" atop a dirt mound, rolled up blueprints in one hand, pointing Moses-like in the distance, and proclaiming that "this is the finest golf course of its kind to be found anywhere in the area."

BEST NEW SHORT FOUR-PAR: 15th hole at the new Tom Fazio Course at Treetops Sylvan Resort, Gaylord, Michigan. A cozy driveable down-hiller through a tightly bunkered driving area to a three-tiered, snaky long green that falls over nine feet (I swear) from front to back. From 80 yards out, the approach can be a knock-down seven-iron, a solid wedge, or a putter.

CLOSEST CLUBHOUSE TO A GREEN: Second hole, 411-yard par-four, Philadelphia Cricket Club, Flourtown, Pennsylvania. A corner of the white stucco clubhouse at this 1922 Tillinghast design sits literally in a greenside bunker, 17 feet from the putting surface.

DAN RATHER AND CONNIE CHUNG GOOD NEWS/BAD NEWS AWARD: University of Michigan Athletic Department. Good news: they've just finished over $1 million in restoration work (with architect Arthur Hills) on their long-neglected Alister MacKenzie-designed campus layout. Now the bad news: they'll continue using the lower section of the course as a parking lot to accommodate the 101,000-seat football stadium across the street. After game day, the 10th fairway looks like a mosh pit.

PETULA CLARK "DOWNTOWN" AWARD: Acapulco GC. Founded circa 1940 and designed by John Brademus and Percy Clifford, it was sadly mangled down to nine holes to make room for a convention center. This unbelievably cramped little layout, the only private club in

town, sits on Acapulco's busiest, nosiest, and filthiest street and overlooks what's left of the beachfront.

PHANTOM GOLF COURSE AWARD: Shadow Creek GC, Las Vegas,
Nevada. Metaphysically speaking, does this thing really exist? Only
in the hyper-real cyberspace of post-modern culture. It's not a resort,
not open to the public, and doesn't have a private membership. In
fact, it's only a Mirage. Nobody gets on the course without going
through Steve Wynn.

SIKORSKY HELICOPTER DROP-SHOT AWARD: Eleventh green at
Bob Cupp's computer-aided-design course, Palmetto Hall on Hilton
Head. The hole is only 315 yards, but the small oxbow-shaped green
wraps around—and behind—a raised frontal bunker and repels any
shot not dropped from above.

BEST DEBUT GOLF COURSE AWARD: Teaching guru Rick Smith's
new course at Treetops Resort in Northern Michigan. Virtually no
earth moved. Smith routed the holes over the softest ground of this
dramatically sloped site. W-i-d-e landing areas. He's not afraid to
build steep contours into his greens, nor to scatter antique bunkers
everywhere. Best hole is the 188-yard par-three 11th, "Sanctuary,"
that was hand cleared through sensitive wetlands and bracken fern.

CHUTZPA AWARD: Cart paths on the new Jack Nicklaus-designed
Monarch Course at Gleneagles Resort in Scotland. And this next to
two fine old James Braid layouts, the Kings and the Queens Courses,
that are cozily routed and easily walked. Predictably, the Monarch offers vertical-walled bunkers, water hazards all of out character with
Scotland, and absurdly long distances between holes. Instead of routing through holes along native glaciated esker ridges, Nicklaus
plowed them over. An unmitigated disaster in every respect.

BEST QUALITY FOR THE BUCK AWARD: Lane Creek GC, a Mike
Young-designed public layout in Watkinsville, Georgia, that opened
in 1993, and cost all of $2.6 million—including the land, roads, and
clubhouse. Fine variety of holes, with plenty of room to miss the ball
and bunker work that respects daily-fee golfers by forcing them to
think.

BEST FUTURE AMERICAN SITE FOR RYDER CUP: Double Eagle,
Tom Weiskopf-Jay Morrish classically-inspired meadowland gem
north of Columbus, Ohio, with massively wide fairways and any
number of pin placements on complexly bunkered greens.

MAD MAN IN THE GARDEN AWARD: Green committees that hire landscape planners who, knowing absolutely nothing about golf, clutter up holes with ornamental trees, formal plantings, and memorial dogwoods. Favorite tricks include small cherry trees in symmetrical rows behind greens, trees inside the line of fairway bunkers, and clusters of midget evergreens as a safety buffer.

WHY ASK WHY? AWARD: Why does the USGA even bother with detailed technical specifications on modern layered greens construction? Winged Foot, Pebble Beach, Shinnecock Hills, Baltusrol, and Inverness all have old-fashioned soil greens. Because of technical constraints, it's basically impossible to build interesting, naturally-flowing contours into a modern spec green.

TIMOTHY LEARY DESIGN TRIP AWARD for renovated hole most out of character with the rest of the course: eighth hole at Scioto CC, Columbus, Ohio. What in the world were Robert Von Hagge, Joe Lee, and Dick Wilson thinking about three decades ago when they blew up the old par-five and built this double forced carry over water hazards, to a peninsula green framed with bulkheads? Donald Ross is still spinning in his grave.

LONGEST WAIT THAT WAS WORTH IT AWARD: Pete Dye Golf Club, Clarksburg, West Virginia. From 1978 to 1993, Pete reportedly made over 150 site visits and spent some $16 million building this thing over an abandoned coal mine. With its exposed coal seam, elevated tee shots across rocky creeks, and a cart path ride through a mine shaft, it is visually overwhelming.

McDONALD'S FAST FOOD DESIGN AWARD: Tour 18 GC in Houston, Texas. Copycat golf courses featuring hamburger versions of filet mignon represent the worst trend in course design.

RESCUE ME AWARD: The old professional's shed behind the first tee at Cruden Bay GC in Scotland. This quaint green wooden building served Cruden Bay for decades, but now sits sadly empty. Somewhere in the world there must be a smart course developer who will buy up this antique building and preserve it.

ENERGIZER BUNNY AWARD: Northern Michigan. They just go on and on up there building new courses. At last count (October 1996), there were 66 new courses growing-in or under construction.

JOEY BUTTAFUCCO "A ROSE BY ANY OTHER NAME" AWARD: French Lick Springs Resort, French Lick, Indiana. A quirky old hotel and a period-piece Donald Ross golf course that sports scarcely a tree. Hosted the 1924 PGA and the 1961 LPGA championships.

WAVEY GRAVEY AWARD: Remember Wavey Gravy, the psychedelic San Francisco hippie who in the late 1960s dispensed drugs from his wildly colored school bus? Seems he's been reincarnated in the form of California-based course architect Robert Muir Graves. How else to explain his trademark Salvador Dali greens and DNA-chain fairways? They're oozing all over the Pacific Northwest. And the beer ad on TV says you can't combine alpine skiing with golf!

EDWARD SCISSORHANDS TOPIARY AWARD: The post-modern designer shrub scheme between the fifth and ninth tees at Tam O'Shanter CC on Long Island, New York. Looks like a collage of nuclear meltdown nerf balls.

BEST TRENDS IN DESIGN AWARD: Squared-off tees, especially on older courses; restoring cross bunkers; caddie programs; 5,000 square foot clubhouses; massive tree removal programs.

FATUOUS NONSENSE AWARD: Golf courses which claim that pull-carts aren't allowed because they convey the wrong look. As if gas-spewing golf cars and wall-to-wall paved paths conveyed a dignified atmosphere.

SOUTHERN COMFORT AWARD: Pine Crest Inn, Pinehurst, North Carolina. Far and away the best golf hotel atmosphere in town, maybe even in the U.S. Creaky old floorboards, historic photographs, favorably priced, a piano bar like no other, and always a few well-lubricated golf writers rolling in the aisles.

SPACE CADET AWARD: 11th hole, Aberdeen GC, Boynton Beach, Florida. This is the infamous "mermaid hole" on a layout that Desmond Muirhead designed to be photographed from the air. It certainly isn't playable on the ground. But who cares, because it looks great—from above.

BULLSEYE ON THE BARN DOOR AWARD: Seventh hole, Langdon Farms GC, Portland, Oregon. Bob Cupp and John Fought have created an appealing public golf course 20 miles south of Portland, just off Route 5. The 548-yard eighth hole is routed alongside an old farm, with the cart path down the left side literally running through a barn. A slight pull off the tee will startle a few chickens out of their roosts.

THEY WENT THATAWAY AWARD: 17th hole, Four Seasons Resort at Aviara, Carlsbad, California. Actually a well-routed course by Ed Seay-Arnold Palmer, but on the long par-five 17th, a directional flag in the second landing zone is about 50 yards right of the target and misleads you into playing into goofy mounds and unplayable ground.

BACK TO BASICS AWARD: Walking Stick GC, Pueblo, Colorado. A lovely municipal layout by Arthur Hills through dry gulch and arroyo country, with green fees at $18 and with most golfers opting to walk.

"AMADEUS" TOO MANY NOTES AWARD: Remember the film where the ignorant prince complains to Mozart that his aria has "too many notes?" The dumbest criticism imaginable. Same goes for those PGA pros whose only gripe about the TPC at River Highlands, Connecticut, site of the Greater Hartford Open, is that the course has "too many bunkers."

JOE ISUZU TRUTH IN ADVERTISING AWARD: The Senior PGA Tour, for its yardages. Maybe their tape measure is about 5 percent off, but these are the shortest-playing 6,700 yard courses in the world. Besides, why shorten the layouts when they're driving the ball longer than they ever did in their "prime" on the PGA Tour? But what should be expected from a Tour that has no cut in order to guarantee the old stars are still around on weekends. The PGA Senior Tour is socialism for aged fat cats.

TIME STANDS STILL AWARD: Kebo Valley Club, Bar Harbor, Maine. A lovely little layout, par-70, 6,112 yards from the back, but who cares about yardage when you've got a rolling, wooded site like this to work with? Natural-looking mounds, intimate greens with interesting rolls, and a 358-yard 17th hole with a legendary yawning dune-bunker 20 feet deep fronting the green.

HAVE YOU READ ANY GOOD GREENS LATELY? AWARD: Most helpful book on course design is Dr. Robert Price's, *Scotland's Golf Courses* (Aberdeen University Press, 1989). A geographer looks at the soil structure and natural history of Scotland's 400+ golf courses and finds, among other things, that only 19 percent of the layouts there are properly classified as seaside "links."

LEONA HELMSLEY-MICHAEL MILKEN GREED AWARD: Operators of Marriott Griffin Gate in Lexington, Kentucky. Let's see, how many homesites can we squeeze onto a golf course? Not content to line the back nine fairways, they blow up the driving range and plant high-density units like weeds. Small wonder they lost a Senior Tour event.

NORTHERN UNDER-EXPOSURE AWARD: Toronto GC in Ontario, Canada. Designed by H.S. Colt in 1912, this gem of a layout on the west side of town retains its period-piece vintage look with lovely red fescue grass framing every shot and an amazing variety of holes. Best of them might be the 339-yard 10th hole, which plays from an elevated tee across a wide minefield of a fairway to a steeply tipped green.

CLASSICAL GAS AWARD: Orchards GC, Washington, Michigan, 30 miles north of Detroit. Designers Robert Trent Jones, Jr. and Don Knott have built a beautiful and demanding public layout that sits 3,000 feet above a vast porous-rock geological formation serving as a natural gas storage facility. The front nine is routed through forest and across streams, while the back nine is on a vast scale reminiscent of C.B. Macdonald.

LOOK BEFORE YOU LEAP AWARD: Pete Dye's PGA Stadium Course, La Quinta, California. Finally got to play this much-maligned layout and loved every inch of it. There's plenty of room to play away from hazards, and if the carries across water are too severe that's because you're playing from the wrong tees.

WOLFMAN JACK AWARD: Wolf Run GC, Zionsville, Indiana. The late Jack Leer had the vision to hire a young Steve Smyers to design a classical looking, fescue-laden layout across rolling ground. Opened in 1989, Wolf Run offers brilliant bunker work, with a wondrous 375-yard opening hole and a back-breaking stretch from the 12th through the 15th. A shame this layout isn't rated among the top-100.

RAY CHARLES SEE THE WHOLE COURSE AWARD: Golfers who can't drive the ball 100 yards but insist on playing from the back tees "to see the whole course" and "play it like the pros." Hey buddy, the pros don't play a 400-yard par-four with a driver, seven-wood, three-iron and two wedge shots. If you want to play it like the pros, play the hole from 350 yards and give yourself a chance to reach the thing with a middle-iron. The best way to experience the full nature of a golf course is to finish out those two-footers instead of conceding putts inside the leather.

NORMAN BATES NO-TELL MOTEL AWARD: *Golf Digest* sure seems "Psycho" when it comes to picking candidates for its 1994 best new "resort course" annual award category: the winner, Pine Barrens at World Woods GC, doesn't have a motel room within 15 miles; same goes for the Links Course at Pelican Hill. Brickyard Crossing GC, adjacent to Indianapolis Speedway, only qualifies because the pro shop is in the basement of a motel. The magazine says it relies upon "the intent" of the owners to build a resort hotel. But then I'm "intent" on making a million dollars a year as a golf writer.

HIDDEN GEM AWARD: Astoria G&CC, Warrenton, Oregon. Known as "The St. Andrews of the Pacific," this runaway stunner sits 85 miles northwest of Portland, a mile off the Pacific Ocean. Created in the mid-1920s by Charles Halderman and George Junor. The holes run parallel through wildly crumpled, corduroy-style sand dunes. Nothing like it in the U.S.

THE PRESTIGIOUS "FIVE HAGGIS" AWARD: Skibo GC, Dornoch, Scotland. A stunning estuarial links by Englishman Donald Steel. The castle, formerly Andrew Carnegie's domicile, offers a unique stay-over, with memorable meals at a massive oak table and each bedroom distinctively furnished. A little steep at 300 pounds sterling per night, but hey, it includes whatever you could ask for or imagine. They'll even shuttle guests to the Inverness airport in a vintage Rolls Royce.

SCARIEST STAT AWARD: "48/100ths of an inch." That's the height of the fairway cut at Indian Summer G&CC, Olympia, Washington. Tough owners, for whom a half-inch isn't good enough. Next thing, they'll be Stimping the bunkers.

ED WOOD's "PLAN 9 FROM OUTER SPACE" AWARD: Talon Course, Grayhawk GC, Scottsdale, Arizona. This grotesquely excessive piece of post-modern office schlock art looks like designers Gary Panks and David Graham set the Terminator Man loose on a CAD-scan and then built to plan. The only thing missing from the bridge to the island tee at the 11th hole is Edvard Munch's "The Scream."

ART MODELL PUBLIC INTEREST AWARD: St. Andrews Links Trust, for its crass sell-off of 7 percent of tee times to some high-priced tour operator. So much for the spirit of linksland. Next we'll see motorized golf carts, laser-yardages, and a neon billboard atop the R&A Clubhouse.

UNSOLVED BRENTWOOD DOUBLE MURDER—VICTIM I: Bel Air CC. Great tunnels, and a classy suspension bridge across the chasm at the 10th hole, but there's no justification for taking out so many great George Thomas bunkers, allowing the double fairway at the

11th hole to grow over, and effacing the greenside mounds at the distinctive "Mae West" 12th hole. The aggravated assault on the old short par-four 9th was particularly grisly. Bad enough that they built a new green, then they had the temerity to create a "championship tee" that requires (I kid you not) a sheer crossfire over the 8th green.

UNSOLVED BRENTWOOD DOUBLE MURDER—Victim II: Los Angeles CC-North Course. The course has gradually lost all too much character, with the worst attack upon the classic drive-and-pitch short par-four 6th hole, sacrificed in order to gain 35 yards on the scorecard.

JUST-IN-TIME AWARD: Hartford GC, West Hartford, Connecticut. Amazing what some well-placed bunkers will do, and just in time to host the 1996 Men's Mid-Amateur. Most of the holes were designed by Devereux Emmet and Donald Ross, then tinkered with and compromised. Now Stephen Kay, superintendent Herb Watson and—believe it or not—the club's green committee have revived/restored it, especially with fairway traps at the dogleg 402-yard 7th and a trio of carry bunkers in the hill at the 231-yard 8th.

NOT IN THE MIDDLE OF NOWHERE AWARD: World Woods GC, Brooksville, Florida. Two distinct new Tom Fazio layouts, with Rolling Oaks a faux Augusta National and Pine Barrens evoking Pine Valley. Not enough to justify the 90-minute drive west of Orlando, Florida? How about a 22-acre circular practice ground, two-acre putting course, and nine-hole short course. Make the trek.

PURE GOLF AWARD: Redtail GC, St. Thomas, Ontario. Co-founders Chris Goodwin and John Drake have evoked all of the game's best sensibilities, including an English-style clubhouse that fronts the 18th fairway. Golf course by Donald Steel is ground-hugging, loaded with texture, and without any tricks. Takes a maximal piece of land to make a minimalist golf course, and this one makes for an idyllic round.

McCULLOUGH CHAINSAW AWARD-VOL. II: Valderrama GC, Cadiz, Spain. No sooner did Ballesteros stop hacking his way around Oak Hill CC-East Course during the '95 Ryder Cup than a battalion of 18-inch blades started firing up here. The only way Seve will be able to play here in the '97 Ryder Cup is if they shave the course down to the turf.

GOLDEN OLDIES AWARD: East Course, Baltimore CC at Five Farms, Timonium, Maryland. A brilliantly natural routing by A.W.

Tillinghast, with bold doglegs and elevation changes on a broad scale, and green contours to match. Amazing, how strong design used to be before earthmoving equipment encouraged designers to level hills and modern greens construction and maintenance made it difficult to sustain dramatic slopes. Superintendent Doug Petersan has done a masterful job of recapturing its subtle terrors.

MUCH ADO ABOUT NOTHING AWARD: Caves Valley Club, Owings Mill, Maryland. A short drive from Five Farms but worlds away in terms of results. All the hype, sanctimonious promotions, and esteemed amateur golf events in the world—not even architect Tom Fazio's reputation—can salvage a bad routing.

BACK-TO-THE-FUTURE AWARD: Southern Dunes GC, Haines City, Florida. Golf started as a public game on firm sandy turf. Okay, this privately-owned daily-fee south of Orlando isn't linksland, but designer Steve Smyers wins high marks for building brilliant strategic shot-making into the tee shots and approaches and for building well-contoured greens that are fun to play.

"THIS MAGIC MOMENT" AWARD: Ben Crenshaw playing the final nine at the '95 Masters. He eyeballed every shot and never once asked caddie Carl Jackson for a yardage. Notice how he played every shot to the high side and let it drift down toward the hole? On the 14th, his wayward drive was redirected by the ghost of Harvey Penick, who quietly moved a tree in the way. Crenshaw's best shot came next, a low-slung eight-iron that rolled just behind the back pin placement. Nobody in golf better understands how to play the lay of the land.

WILE E. COYOTE AWARD: Oasis GC, Mesquite, Nevada. Road Runner meets Blade Runner. Owners Si Redd and Dennis Rider are sitting on a dry as bones mesa that's turning into a land-mine casino and real estate development, with a second 18-hole course by Arnold Palmer and Ed Seay underway. This one is cut through wild terrain. Typical Arnie: where nature didn't provide a landing area, they just bulldozed like all hell, planted tees on outcrops, and have you fire away. Know what? It works.

STATE OF THE NATION AWARD: Oregon is a runaway winner when it comes to quality public golf. Recent standouts include three courses by Bob Cupp and John Fought: Langdon Farms south of Portland, Ghost Creek C. at Pumpkin Ridge, and the new Crosswater layout at Sunriver Resort amid the mountains of Bend. The Jones boys have lately gotten into the act as well, with Rees' Sandpines along the coastline and Bobby's latest, Eagle Point, north of Medford, open as well. Perhaps the state's course and resort owners will someday mount a national (and not just a west coast) promo campaign.

BEST TREND AWARD: Green contours are back. As a result of steadily increasing greens speeds, architects had been retreating from interesting green contours. The terminal point was the comatose flat-line of Colleton River's putting surfaces. Four new layouts may help reverse that trend: Rick Smith's course at Treetops Resort, Michigan; Crenshaw-Coore's stunning Sand Hills in Mullen, Nebraska (best natural green sites in the USA); the Pete Dye GC in Bridgeport, West Virginia; and the Pete Dye-Greg Norman designed Medalist Club in Hobe Sound, Florida. The trick in building roly-poly greens is getting the putting surfaces large enough and then providing containment. The Medalist can be faulted on this latter point, but the results are still a whole lot more interesting than vanilla bland design.

GOLDEN HAGGIS AWARD: New Course, Grand Cypress Resort, Orlando, Florida. Nobody did more to undermine classical design values than the Jack Nicklaus of the 1980s. And yet in the midst of a period devoted to garish excesses comes this joyously playable ode to the Old Course as a centerpiece of one of the country's most financially successful (i.e., expensive) golf resorts. The "faux" St. Andrews holes are loads of fun to play, the fairways are wide enough for a tank division to practice maneuvers, and the revetted bunkers and seven double greens (some with six-foot contours) are bold to the extreme. Bonus points for the perfectly executed side-by-side versions of the original 1st and 18th holes.

For Further Reading

Balfour, James. 1887. *Reminiscences of Golf on St. Andrews Links*. Edinburgh: David Douglas.

Browning, Robert. 1955. *A History of Golf: The Royal and Ancient Game*. London: J.M. Dent & Sons Ltd.

Christian, Frank with Cal Brown. 1996. *Augusta National and The Masters: A Photographer's Sketchbook*. Chelsea, Michigan: Sleeping Bear Press.

Colt, H.S. and C.H. Alison. 1920. *Some Essays on Golf Course Architecture*. New York: Charles Scribner's Sons.

Cornish, Geoffrey S. and Ronald E. Whitten. 1993. *The Architects of Golf*. New York: HarperCollins.

Darwin, Bernard. 1910. *The Golf Courses of the British Isles*. London: Duckworth & Company.

Darwin, Bernard. 1944. *Golf Between Two Wars*. London: Chatto & Windus.

Doak, Tom. 1992. *The Anatomy of a Golf Course: The Art of Golf Architecture*. New York: Lyons & Burford.

Doak, Tom. 1996. *The Confidential Guide to Golf Courses*. Chelsea, Michigan: Sleeping Bear Press.

Dye, Pete with Mark Shaw. 1995. *Bury Me in a Pot Bunker*. Reading, Massachusetts. New York: Addison Wesley.

Hawtree, F.W. 1983. *The Golf Course: Planning, Design, Construction and Maintenance*. London: E.& F.N. Spon.

Hiss, Tony. 1991. *The Experience of Place*. New York: Vintage.

Hunter, Robert. 1926. *The Links*. New York: Charles Scribner's Sons.

Hurdzan, Michael. 1996. *Golf Course Architecture: Design, Construction and Restoration*. Chelsea, Michigan: Sleeping Bear Press.

Jenkins, Virginia Scott. 1994. *The Lawn: A History of an American Obsession*. Washington, D.C.: Smithsonian Institution Press.

Jones, Rees and Guy Rando. 1974. *Golf Course Developments*. Washington, D.C.: Urban Land Institute.

Jones, Robert Trent and Larry Dennis. 1988. *Golf's Magnificent Challenge*. New York: McGraw-Hill.

Jones, Robert Trent, Jr. 1993. *Golf by Design*. Boston: Little, Brown.

Kunstler, William Howard. 1991. *The Geography of Nowhere*. New York: Oxford University Press.

Macdonald, Charles Blair. 1928. *Scotland's Gift: Golf.* New York: Charles Scribner's Sons.

MacKenzie, Alister. 1920. *Golf Architecture.* London: Simpkin, Marshall, Hamilton, Kent & Company.

MacKenzie, Alister. 1995. *The Spirit of St. Andrews.* Chelsea, Michigan: Sleeping Bear Press.

Moore, Charles W., William J. Mitchell, and William Turnbull, Jr. 1991. *The Poetics of Gardens.* Cambridge, Massachusetts: MIT Press.

Pollan, Michael. 1991. *Second Nature: A Gardener's Education.* New York: Atlantic Monthly Press.

Price, Robert. 1989. *Scotland's Golf Courses.* Aberdeen: Aberdeen University Press.

Raitz, Karl B., ed. 1995. *The Theater of Sport.* Baltimore, Maryland: Johns Hopkins University Press.

Ross, Donald. 1996. *Golf Has Never Failed Me.* Chelsea, Michigan: Sleeping Bear Press.

Rubenstein, Lorne. 1990. *Links: An Insider's Tour Through the World of Golf.* Toronto: Random House.

Shackelford, Geoff. 1995. *Riviera Country Club: A Definitive History.* Pacific Palisades, California: Riviera Country Club.

Shackelford, Geoff. 1996. *The Captain: George C. Thomas Jr. and His Golf Architecture.* Chelsea, Michigan: Captain Fantastic Publishing/Sleeping Bear Press.

Steel, Donald. 1992. *Classic Golf Links of England, Scotland, Wales, and Ireland.* Gretna, Louisiana: Pelican Publishing.

Strawn, John. 1991. *Driving the Green: The Making of a Golf Course.* New York: HarperCollins.

Thomas, George C., Jr. 1927. *Golf Architecture in America: Its Strategy and Construction.* Los Angeles: The Times-Mirror Press.

Tillinghast, A.W. 1996. *The Course Beautiful: A Collection of Original Articles and Photographs on Golf Course Design.* Warren, New Jersey: TreeWolf Productions. (888-580-8455)

Ward-Thomas, Pat, et al. 1976. *The World Atlas of Golf: The Great Courses and How They Are Played.* New York: Gallery Books.

Ward-Thomas, Pat. 1990. *The Lay of the Land.* New York: Ailsa, Inc.

Wethered, H.N. and T. Simpson. 1929. *The Architectural Side of Golf.* London: Longmans, Green & Co.

Wind, Herbert Warren. 1985. *Following Through.* New York: Ticknor & Fields.

Zukin, Sharon. 1991. *Landscapes of Power: From Detroit to Disney World.* Berkeley, California: University of California Press.